AMERICA'S FAVORITES™

Holiday

pil

Publications International, Ltd.

Favorite Brand Name Recipes at www.fbnr.com

Pictured on the front cover: Pesto Cheese Wreath *(page 25).*
Pictured on the back cover *(left to right):* Crown Roast of Pork with Peach Stuffing
(page 58) and Fried Norwegian Cookies (Fattigmandbakkelse) *(page 146).*

Microwave Cooking: Microwave ovens vary in wattage. Use the cooking times as guidelines
and check for doneness before adding more time.

Preparation/Cooking Times: Preparation times are based on the approximate amount of
time required to assemble the recipe before cooking, baking, chilling or serving. These times
include preparation steps such as measuring, chopping and mixing. The fact that some
preparations and cooking can be done simultaneously is taken into account. Preparation of
optional ingredients and serving suggestions is not included.

Table of Contents

Holiday Star
page 16

Fried Norwegian Cookies (Fattigmandbakkelse)
page 146

Quick Pickled Green Beans

½ pound (3 ½ cups loosely packed) whole green beans

½ red bell pepper, cut into strips (optional)

1 jalapeño* or other hot pepper, cut into strips

1 large clove garlic, cut in half

1 bay leaf

1 cup white wine vinegar

1 cup water

½ cup white wine

1 tablespoon sugar

1 tablespoon salt

1 tablespoon whole coriander seeds

1 tablespoon mustard seeds

1 tablespoon whole peppercorns

Jalapeño peppers can sting and irritate the skin. Wear rubber gloves when handling and do not touch eyes.

1. Wash green beans and remove stem ends. Place in glass dish just large enough to hold green beans and 2½ cups liquid. Add bell pepper strips, if desired. Tuck jalapeño, garlic and bay leaf between beans.

2. Place remaining ingredients in medium saucepan. Heat to a boil; stir to dissolve sugar and salt. Reduce heat; simmer 5 minutes. Pour mixture over green beans, making sure beans are submerged in liquid. If not, add additional hot water to cover.

3. Cover; refrigerate at least 24 hours. Remove and discard bay leaf before serving. Flavor improves in 48 hours and beans may be kept refrigerated for up to five days. Remove beans from liquid before serving.   *Makes 6 appetizer servings*

Quick Pickled Green Beans

Beefy Pinwheels

- 1 package (8 ounces) cream cheese
- 1/4 cup chopped pimiento-stuffed green olives
- 2 tablespoons prepared horseradish mustard
- 6 (6- to 7-inch) flour tortillas
- 12 small slices deli roast beef
- 6 green onions, tops included

1. Place unwrapped cream cheese on paper plate. Microwave at HIGH 15 seconds or until softened. Combine cream cheese, olives and mustard in small bowl; mix well.

2. Spread about 2 tablespoons cream cheese mixture over each tortilla. Top each with 2 overlapping slices of beef.

3. Place onion on one edge of tortilla, trimming onion to fit diameter of tortilla. Roll up tortilla jelly-roll fashion. Cut each roll into slices to serve.   *Makes 6 servings*

Vegetable Hummus

- 2 cloves garlic
- 2 cans (15 to 19 ounces each) chickpeas or garbanzo beans, rinsed and drained
- 1 package KNORR® Recipe Classics™ Vegetable Soup, Dip and Recipe Mix
- 1/2 cup water
- 1/2 cup BERTOLLI® Olive Oil
- 2 tablespoons lemon juice
- 1/4 teaspoon ground cumin
- 6 (8-inch) whole wheat or white pita breads, cut into wedges

✦ In food processor, pulse garlic until finely chopped. Add remaining ingredients except pita bread. Process until smooth; chill at least 2 hours.

✦ Stir hummus before serving. If desired, add 1 to 2 tablespoons additional olive oil, or to taste. Serve with pita wedges.   *Makes 3 1/2 cups dip*

Beefy Pinwheels

Ginger-Lemon Cheese Spread with Pineapple-Peach Sauce

2 packages (8 ounces each) cream cheese, softened

1 cup sour cream

3 tablespoons packed brown sugar

1 tablespoon grated lemon peel

3/4 teaspoon ground ginger

1/2 cup crushed pineapple, well drained

1/2 cup peach or apricot preserves

Assorted crackers and fresh fruit

1. Line 3-cup decorative mold or bowl with plastic wrap.

2. Combine cream cheese and sour cream in large bowl; beat until creamy. (Do not overbeat.) Add brown sugar, lemon peel and ginger; stir until well blended.

3. Spoon cheese mixture into prepared mold. Cover with plastic wrap; refrigerate at least 8 hours or up to 2 days.

4. To complete recipe, combine pineapple and peach preserves in small bowl. Unmold cheese spread onto serving plate. Spoon sauce around cheese. Serve with crackers and fruit.   *Makes 8 servings*

Variation: Press toasted chopped walnuts onto cheese spread and serve Pineapple-Peach Sauce alongside of spread.

Make-Ahead Time: Up to 2 days before serving ✦ *Final Prep Time*: 5 minutes

8

Ginger-Lemon Cheese Spread with
Pineapple-Peach Sauce

Shrimp Spread

½ pound medium shrimp, peeled and deveined, reserving shells

1 cup water

½ teaspoon onion powder

½ teaspoon garlic salt

1 package (8 ounces) cream cheese, softened

¼ cup (½ stick) butter, softened

2 tablespoons mayonnaise

2 tablespoons cocktail sauce

1 tablespoon lemon juice

1 tablespoon chopped fresh parsley

Assorted crackers or raw vegetables

Green onion, star fruit, kiwi fruit and radish slices for garnish

1. Place reserved shrimp shells, water, onion powder and garlic salt in medium saucepan. Bring to a simmer over medium heat; simmer 5 minutes. Remove shells and discard. Add shrimp; simmer 1 minute or until shrimp turn pink and opaque. Remove shrimp to cutting board; let cool. Continue cooking shrimp liquid; reduce to about 3 tablespoons.

2. Blend cream cheese, butter, mayonnaise, cocktail sauce and lemon juice in large bowl until smooth. Stir in 1 tablespoon reduced cooking liquid. Discard remaining liquid.

3. Finely chop shrimp. Fold shrimp and parsley into cheese mixture.

4. Pack spread into decorative serving crock or mold lined with plastic wrap. Cover; refrigerate overnight. Serve spread in crock or invert mold onto serving platter; remove plastic wrap. Serve with crackers or vegetables. Garnish, if desired.

Makes 2½ to 3 cups

Shrimp Spread

Stuffed Mushrooms

24 fresh medium mushrooms (about 1 pound)

6 ounces boneless lean pork

1/4 cup whole water chestnuts (1/4 of 8-ounce can)

3 green onions with tops

1/2 small red or green bell pepper

1 small rib celery

2 teaspoons dry sherry

1 teaspoon cornstarch

1 teaspoon minced fresh ginger

1 teaspoon soy sauce

1/2 teaspoon hoisin sauce

1 egg white, lightly beaten

Vegetable oil for frying

1/2 cup all-purpose flour

Batter (page 14)

Fresh thyme leaves for garnish

1. Remove stems from mushrooms; set caps aside. Chop stems finely and transfer to large bowl.

2. Finely chop pork, water chestnuts, onions, bell pepper and celery. Add to chopped mushroom stems. Add sherry, cornstarch, ginger, soy sauce, hoisin sauce and egg white; mix well.

3. Spoon pork mixture into mushroom caps, mounding slightly in center.

4. Dip mushrooms into flour, then into batter, coating completely.

5. Add six to eight mushrooms to hot oil; cook about 5 minutes or until golden brown on all sides. Drain on paper towels. Repeat with remaining mushrooms. Garnish, if desired.

Makes 2 dozen

continued on page 14

12

13

Stuffed Mushrooms

Stuffed Mushrooms, *continued*

Batter

- ¹/₂ **cup cornstarch**
- ¹/₂ **cup all-purpose flour**
- 1 ¹/₂ **teaspoons baking powder**
- ³/₄ **teaspoon salt**
- ¹/₃ **cup water**
- ¹/₃ **cup milk**

Combine cornstarch, flour, baking powder and salt in medium bowl. Add water and milk; stir until well blended.

Easy Cheese Fondue

- 1 **pound low-sodium Swiss cheese (Gruyère, Emmentaler or combination of both), divided**
- 2 **tablespoons cornstarch**
- 1 **garlic clove, crushed**
- 1 **cup HOLLAND HOUSE® White or White with Lemon Cooking Wine**
- 1 **tablespoon kirsch or cherry brandy (optional)**
  Pinch nutmeg
  Ground black pepper

1. In medium bowl, coat cheese with cornstarch; set aside. Rub inside of ceramic fondue pot or heavy saucepan with garlic; discard garlic. Bring wine to gentle simmer over medium heat. Gradually stir in cheese to ensure smooth fondue. Once smooth, stir in brandy, if desired. Garnish with nutmeg and pepper.

2. Serve with bite-sized chunks of French bread, broccoli, cauliflower, tart apples or pears. Spear with fondue forks or wooden skewers. *Makes 1 ¹/₄ cups*

14

15

Easy Cheese Fondue

Holiday Star

TOPPING
3/4 cup sour cream

1/2 cup mayonnaise

2 tablespoons heavy cream

1 teaspoon balsamic vinegar

1/4 cup chopped fresh cilantro

1/4 cup chopped fresh basil

1/4 cup chopped roasted red peppers, drained and patted dry

1/2 teaspoon garlic powder

1/4 teaspoon salt

Black pepper to taste

STAR
2 cans (8 ounces each) refrigerated crescent roll dough

GARNISHES
Red bell pepper, chopped

Green onion, chopped

Black olive slices (optional)

1. Preheat oven to 375°F.

2. Combine sour cream, mayonnaise, heavy cream and balsamic vinegar in medium bowl. Stir in cilantro, basil and roasted red peppers. Add garlic powder, salt and black pepper; mix well. Cover and refrigerate at least 1 hour to let flavors blend.

3. Place 2-inch round cookie cutter or similar size custard cup in center of 14-inch pizza pan; set aside. Remove dough from first can; unroll on cookie sheet. Seal perforations by pressing down slightly with fingers. Cut 24 circles with 1 1/2-inch cookie cutter. Remove excess dough from cut circles; set aside. Repeat with second can.

4. Evenly space five dough circles around outside edge of pizza pan. (These will be the star points.) From each star point, make a triangle pattern with rows of slightly overlapping dough circles, working toward cookie cutter in center of pan. (See photo.) Roll excess dough into ball; flatten with hands. Cut more circles as needed to completely fill star.

continued on page 18

16

Holiday Star

Holiday Star, *continued*

5. Remove cookie cutter from center of star. Bake 12 to 16 minutes or until star is light golden brown. Cool completely, in pan on wire rack, about 30 minutes.

6. Spread topping over star. Garnish with red bell pepper, green onion and black olives, if desired. Place decorative candle in center of star. Serve immediately.

Makes about 16 servings

Helpful Hint: For a festive garnish, hollow out a red or green bell pepper and fill it with any remaining dip. Place fresh vegetables, such as broccoli florets or bell pepper strips, around the star.

Baked Garlic Bundles

½ **(16-ounce) package frozen phyllo dough, thawed to room temperature**
¾ **cup (1½ sticks) butter, melted**
3 **large heads garlic,* separated into cloves and peeled**
½ **cup finely chopped walnuts**
1 **cup Italian-style bread crumbs**

**The whole garlic bulb is called a head.*

1. Preheat oven to 350°F. Remove phyllo from package; unroll and place on large sheet of waxed paper. Using scissors, cut phyllo crosswise into 2-inch-wide strips. Cover with large sheet of waxed paper and damp kitchen towel. (Phyllo dries out quickly if not covered.)

2. Lay 1 phyllo strip on flat surface; brush immediately with melted butter. Place 1 clove garlic at end of strip. Sprinkle about 1 teaspoon walnuts over length of strip. Roll up garlic clove and walnuts in strip, tucking in side edges while rolling. Brush bundle with melted butter; roll in bread crumbs to coat. Repeat with remaining phyllo strips, garlic cloves, walnuts, butter and bread crumbs until all but smallest garlic cloves are used. Place bundles on rack in shallow roasting pan. Bake 20 minutes or until crispy.

Makes about 2 dozen appetizers

19

Baked Garlic Bundles

Swedish-Style Meatballs

4 tablespoons butter, divided

1 cup minced onion

1 pound 90% lean ground beef

1/2 pound ground veal

1/2 pound ground pork

1 cup fresh bread crumbs

2 eggs, lightly beaten

1/2 teaspoon salt

1/4 teaspoon black pepper

1/8 teaspoon grated nutmeg

1 1/4 cups milk

1/4 cup half-and-half

1 egg yolk

1/2 teaspoon salt

3 tablespoons all-purpose flour

1. Melt 2 tablespoons butter in large skillet over medium heat. Add onion. Cook and stir 8 to 10 minutes or until onions are very soft. Remove from heat; set aside. Combine beef, veal, pork, bread crumbs, beaten eggs, salt, pepper and nutmeg in large bowl. Add onions; mix well. Use 1 tablespoon meat mixture; shape into balls. Set aside.

2. Preheat oven to 200°F.

3. Reheat skillet over medium heat. Add 1/4 to 1/3 of meatballs. Do not crowd pan. Cook 8 minutes, shaking pan to allow meatballs to roll and brown evenly. Reduce heat to medium-low. Cook 15 to 20 minutes or until cooked through. Transfer to covered casserole dish and keep warm in oven. Repeat until all meatballs are cooked.

4. Meanwhile, combine milk, half-and-half, egg yolk and salt in small bowl. Wipe out skillet. Melt remaining 2 tablespoons butter over medium heat. Whisk in flour. Stir well. Slowly stir into flour mixture. Reduce heat to medium-low. Cook and stir 3 minutes or until thickened. Remove dish from oven and pour sauce over meatballs. Serve immediately. *Makes 72 cocktail-size meatballs*

Swedish-Style Meatballs

Shrimp Tapas in Sherry Sauce

1 slice thick-cut bacon, cut into ¼-inch strips (optional)

2 tablespoons olive oil

2 ounces crimini or button mushrooms, sliced into quarters

½ pound large shrimp (about 16 shrimp), peeled and deveined, leaving tails attached

2 cloves garlic, thinly sliced

2 tablespoons medium dry sherry

1 tablespoon fresh lemon juice

¼ teaspoon red pepper flakes

1. Cook bacon in large skillet over medium heat until brown and crispy. Remove from skillet with slotted spoon and drain on paper towels. Set aside.

2. Add oil to bacon drippings in skillet. Add mushrooms; cook and stir 2 minutes.

3. Add shrimp and garlic; cook and stir 3 minutes or until shrimp turn pink and opaque. Stir in sherry, lemon juice and red pepper flakes.

4. Remove shrimp to serving bowl with slotted spoon. Cook sauce 1 minute or until reduced and thickened. Pour over shrimp. Sprinkle with reserved bacon.

Makes 4 appetizer servings

Tips to share

Tapas are Spanish appetizers that are served in bars and restaurants to stave off hunger until the late evening Spanish dinner. These dishes range from something as simple as a cube of cheese to more elaborate preparations, such as cold potato omelets and shrimp cooked in sherry sauce.

23

Shrimp Tapas in Sherry Sauce

Tuna and Olive Spread

1 (3-ounce) pouch of **STARKIST** Flavor Fresh Pouch® Albacore or Chunk
   Light Tuna

1 hard-cooked egg *or* 2 hard-cooked egg whites

1/2 cup soft cream cheese

1/4 cup prepared green onion dip

1 can (4 1/4 ounces) chopped ripe olives

   Salt and black pepper to taste

   Snipped chives and paprika, for garnish

   Crackers, assorted breads or raw vegetables

In food processor bowl with metal blade, place tuna, egg, cream cheese and onion dip; process until smooth. Transfer to bowl; stir in olives, salt and pepper. Chill several hours or overnight before serving. Mold into special shape, if desired. Garnish with chives and paprika. Serve with crackers.   *Makes about 12 servings*

Prep Time: 5 minutes

Original Ranch® Meatballs

1 pound ground beef

1 packet (1 ounce) **HIDDEN VALLEY®** The Original Ranch® Salad Dressing
   & Seasoning Mix

2 tablespoons butter or margarine

1/2 cup beef broth

Combine ground beef and salad dressing & seasoning mix. Shape into meatballs. Melt butter in a skillet; brown meatballs on all sides. Add broth; cover and simmer 10 to 15 minutes or until cooked through. Serve warm with toothpicks.

Makes 2 dozen meatballs

24

Pesto Cheese Wreath

Parsley-Basil Pesto (recipe follows)
3 **packages (8 ounces each) cream cheese, softened**
1/2 **cup mayonnaise**
1/4 **cup whipping cream or half-and-half**
1 **teaspoon sugar**
1 **teaspoon onion salt**
1/3 **cup chopped pimiento, drained**
Pimiento strips and Italian flat leaf parsley leaves (optional)
Assorted crackers and cut-up vegetables

1. Prepare Parsley-Basil Pesto; set aside. Beat cream cheese and mayonnaise in medium bowl until smooth; beat in whipping cream, sugar and onion salt.

2. Line 5-cup ring mold with plastic wrap. Spoon half of cheese mixture into prepared mold; spread evenly. Spread Parsley-Basil Pesto evenly over cheese mixture; top with chopped pimiento. Spread remaining cheese mixture evenly over peppers. Cover; refrigerate until cheese mixture is firm, 8 hours or overnight.

3. Uncover mold; invert onto serving plate. Carefully remove plastic wrap. Smooth top and sides of wreath with spatula. Garnish with pimiento strips and parsley, if desired. Serve with crackers and vegetables.   *Makes 16 to 24 appetizer servings*

Parsley-Basil Pesto

2 **cups fresh parsley leaves**
1/4 **cup pine nuts or slivered almonds**
2 **tablespoons grated Parmesan cheese**
2 **cloves garlic, peeled**
1 **tablespoon dried basil leaves, crushed**
1/4 **teaspoon salt**
2 **tablespoons olive or vegetable oil**

Process all ingredients except oil in food processor or blender until finely chopped. With machine running, add oil gradually, processing until mixture is smooth.

Makes about 1/2 cup

Turkey Meatballs in Cranberry-Barbecue Sauce

- 1 can (16 ounces) jellied cranberry sauce
- 1/2 cup barbecue sauce
- 1 egg white
- 1 pound 93% lean ground turkey
- 1 green onion with top, sliced
- 2 teaspoons grated orange peel
- 1 teaspoon reduced-sodium soy sauce
- 1/4 teaspoon black pepper
- 1/8 teaspoon ground red pepper (optional)

Slow Cooker Directions

1. Combine cranberry and barbecue sauces in slow cooker. Cover; cook on HIGH 20 to 30 minutes or until cranberry sauce is melted and mixture is hot.

2. Meanwhile, place egg white in medium bowl; beat lightly. Add turkey, green onion, orange peel, soy sauce, black pepper and ground red pepper, if desired; mix well with hands until well blended. Shape into 24 balls.

3. Spray large nonstick skillet with nonstick cooking spray. Add meatballs to skillet; cook over medium heat 8 to 10 minutes or until meatballs are no longer pink in center, carefully turning occasionally to brown evenly. Add to heated sauce in slow cooker; stir gently to coat.

4. Reduce heat to LOW. Cover; cook 3 hours. Transfer meatballs to serving plate; garnish, if desired. Serve with decorative picks.   *Makes 12 servings*

Turkey Meatballs in Cranberry-Barbecue Sauce

Marinated Antipasto Kabobs

1/2 **(9-ounce)** package spinach three-cheese tortellini or plain tortellini

1 package **(9 ounces)** frozen artichoke hearts, thawed

20 small fresh mushrooms, stems removed

1 large red bell pepper, cut into 20 equal-sized pieces

1/2 cup white balsamic or white wine vinegar

1/4 cup grated Parmesan cheese

1/4 cup minced fresh basil

2 tablespoons Dijon mustard

1 tablespoon olive oil

1/2 teaspoon sugar

1/4 teaspoon black pepper

20 cherry tomatoes

1. Cook tortellini according to package directions. Drain well. Cool slightly; cover and refrigerate until ready to assemble kabobs.

2. Cook artichokes according to package directions; drain. Immediately add artichokes to bowl of ice water to stop cooking process. Let stand 1 to 2 minutes; drain well. Place artichokes in large resealable plastic food storage bag. Add mushrooms and bell pepper.

3. Combine vinegar, cheese, basil, mustard, oil, sugar and black pepper in small bowl; mix well. Add to vegetable mixture in plastic bag; seal bag. Turn bag over several times to coat ingredients evenly. Refrigerate several hours or overnight, turning bag occasionally.

4. Remove vegetables from marinade, reserving marinade. Arrange vegetables on skewers alternately with tortellini and tomatoes; place on serving platter. Drizzle with reserved marinade, if desired. *Makes 20 kabobs*

Note: Don't clean mushrooms until just before you're ready to use them (they will absorb water and become mushy). Wipe them with a damp paper towel or rinse them under cold running water and blot dry.

29

Marinated Antipasto Kabobs

Wassail Bowl

Ingredients

Dried apple slices

Colored sugar

3/4 cup water

3/4 cup granulated sugar

1/2 teaspoon ground ginger

1/4 teaspoon ground nutmeg

1 small cinnamon stick

3 whole cloves

3 whole allspice

3 coriander seeds

3 cardamom seeds (optional)

3 cups ale or wine

2 1/4 cups dry sherry

1/3 cup cognac

Supplies

Tiny cookie cutters

1. Using tiny cookie cutters or sharp knife, cut dried apple slices into festive shapes; moisten with water and coat with colored sugar. Set aside.

2. Combine 3/4 cup water, granulated sugar and spices in large saucepan. Bring to a boil. Cover; reduce heat and simmer 5 minutes.

3. Stir in ale, sherry and cognac; heat just to simmering. Do not boil. Strain into heatproof pitcher or punch bowl. Float apple slices in punch.

Makes 12 servings (about 4 ounces each)

Wassail Bowl

Piña Colada Punch

5 cups DOLE® Pineapple Juice, divided
1 can (15 ounces) real cream of coconut
1 liter lemon-lime soda
2 limes
1 ½ cups light rum (optional)
   Ice cubes
   Mint sprigs

✦ Chill all ingredients.

✦ Blend 2 cups pineapple juice with cream of coconut in blender. Combine puréed mixture with remaining 3 cups pineapple juice, soda, juice of 1 lime, rum and ice. Garnish with 1 sliced lime and mint sprigs.
Makes 15 servings

32

Spiced Orange Tea

3 cups water
1 cup orange juice
2 tablespoons lemon juice
¼ cup sugar
1 cinnamon stick
½ teaspoon whole cloves
2 tea bags
   Ice cubes (optional)
   Mint sprigs (optional)

Combine water, juices, sugar, cinnamon stick, cloves and tea bags in 2-quart saucepan. Cook over medium heat, stirring occasionally, until sugar is dissolved. Cover pan when mixture just begins to steam. Turn off heat; let steep 5 minutes. Strain tea into preheated teapot; serve hot. Or, to serve cold, strain tea into 1 ½-quart container with tight-fitting lid. Cover when cool and refrigerate until very cold. Serve in ice-filled tumblers. Garnish each serving with mint.
Makes 4 servings

33

Piña Colada Punch

Champagne Punch

1 orange

1 lemon

¼ cup cranberry-flavored liqueur or cognac

¼ cup orange-flavored liqueur or Triple Sec

1 bottle (750 mL) pink or regular champagne or sparkling white wine, well chilled

Fresh cranberries (optional)

Citrus strips for garnish

1. Remove colored peel, not white pith, from orange and lemon in long thin strips with citrus peeler. Refrigerate orange and lemon for another use. Combine peels and cranberry- and orange-flavored liqueurs in glass pitcher. Cover and refrigerate 2 to 6 hours.

2. Just before serving, tilt pitcher to one side and slowly pour in champagne. Leave peels in pitcher for added flavor. Place 1 cranberry in bottom of each champagne glass, if desired. Pour punch into glasses. Garnish with citrus strips tied in knots.

Makes 4 cups (6 to 8 servings)

Nonalcoholic Cranberry Punch: Pour 3 cups well-chilled club soda into ⅔ cup (6 ounces) cranberry cocktail concentrate, thawed. Makes 3½ cups (6 servings).

Apple Snow

1½ cups MOTT'S® Apple Juice

1 tablespoon honey

3 cups ice

Place apple juice, honey and ice in blender; blend until finely crushed or to consistency of snow. Serve immediately.

Makes 2 servings

34

Champagne Punch

Snowbird Mocktails

3 cups pineapple juice
1 can (14 ounces) sweetened condensed milk
1 can (6 ounces) frozen orange juice concentrate, thawed
½ teaspoon coconut extract
1 bottle (32 ounces) ginger ale, chilled

1. Combine pineapple juice, sweetened condensed milk, orange juice concentrate and coconut extract in large pitcher; stir well. Cover; refrigerate at least 1 hour or up to 1 week.

2. To serve, pour ½ cup pineapple juice mixture into individual glasses (over crushed ice, if desired). Top off each glass with about ⅓ cup ginger ale. Garnish as desired.

Makes 10 servings

Tip: Store unopened cans of sweetened condensed milk at room temperature up to 6 months. Once opened, store in airtight container in refrigerator for up to 5 days.

Prep Time: 10 minutes

36

Holiday Egg Nog Punch

2 (1-quart) cans BORDEN® Egg Nog, chilled
1 (12-ounce) can frozen orange juice concentrate, thawed
1 cup cold water
Orange sherbet

1. In large pitcher combine all ingredients except sherbet; mix well.

2. Just before serving, pour into punch bowl; top with scoops of sherbet. Refrigerate leftovers.

Makes about 1 quart

Prep Time: 5 minutes

Snowbird Mocktails

Hot Mulled Cider

1 orange

1 lemon

12 whole cloves

6 cups apple cider

1/3 cup sugar

3 cinnamon sticks

12 whole allspice berries

Poke 6 evenly spaced holes in a ring around orange and lemon with point of wooden skewer. Insert whole cloves into holes. Cut slice out of orange to include all cloves. Cut remainder of orange into thin slices. Repeat procedure with lemon. Combine all ingredients in medium saucepan. Bring just to a simmer over medium heat. Do not boil. Reduce heat to low; cook 5 minutes. Pour cider through strainer into mugs. Discard fruit and seasonings. Garnish as desired.   *Makes 6 cups*

38

White Sangria

1 carton (64 ounces) DOLE® Pineapple Orange Banana Juice

2 cups fruity white wine

2 cups sliced DOLE® Fresh Strawberries

1 orange, thinly sliced

1 lime, thinly sliced

1/4 cup sugar

1/4 cup orange-flavored liqueur

Ice cubes

Mint sprigs for garnish

Combine juice, wine, strawberries, orange, lime, sugar and liqueur in 2 large pitchers; cover and refrigerate 2 hours to blend flavors. Serve over ice. Garnish with mint sprigs.   *Makes 20 servings*

39

Hot Mulled Cider

Cranberry-Lime Margarita Punch

6 cups water
1 container (12 ounces) frozen cranberry juice cocktail
1/2 cup fresh lime juice
1/4 cup sugar
2 cups ice cubes
1 cup ginger ale or tequila
1 lime, sliced

1. Combine water, juices and sugar in punch bowl; stir until sugar dissolves.

2. Stir in ice cubes and ginger ale; garnish each serving with fresh cranberries and lime slice, if desired.

Makes 10 (8-ounce) servings

Wisconsin Spicy Apple Eggnog

3 cups milk
2 cups light cream or half-and-half
2 beaten eggs*
1/3 cup sugar
1/2 teaspoon ground cinnamon
Dash salt
3/4 cup apple brandy
Ground nutmeg

*Use clean, uncracked eggs.

In large saucepan combine milk, light cream, eggs, sugar, cinnamon and salt. Cook and stir over medium heat until mixture is slightly thickened and heated through. Do not boil. Remove from heat; stir in apple brandy. To serve, ladle mixture into 12 heatproof glasses or cups. Sprinkle each serving with nutmeg. Serve warm.

Makes 12 servings

Prep Time: 25 minutes

Favorite recipe from **Wisconsin Milk Marketing Board**

41

Cranberry-Lime Margarita Punch

Holiday Orange Eggnog

1 container (8 ounces) refrigerated egg substitute to equal 4 eggs (1 cup)

1/3 cup sugar

2 teaspoons ground nutmeg

1/4 teaspoon ground cinnamon

2 cups cold milk

1 pint regular or low-fat frozen vanilla yogurt, softened

Juice of 3 SUNKIST® oranges (1 cup), chilled

1/2 to 1 cup rum, bourbon or brandy (or any combination)

Freshly grated SUNKIST® orange peel

Additional ground nutmeg

In large bowl, combine egg substitute, sugar, 2 teaspoons nutmeg and cinnamon; whisk well to dissolve sugar. Whisk in milk, yogurt, orange juice and rum. (If made ahead and chilled, whisk well before serving.) Garnish each serving with orange peel and dash of nutmeg.

Makes about 6 cups, 8 (6-ounce) or 12 (4-ounce) servings

42

Slow Burn Martini

2 ounces premium vodka

1/2 ounce vermouth

5 drops TABASCO® brand Pepper Sauce

1 slice jalapeño pepper

Place 4 to 5 ice cubes in cocktail shaker. Pour vodka and vermouth over ice; cover and shake. Strain into chilled martini glass. Stir in TABASCO® Sauce; garnish with jalapeño.

Makes 1 martini

Pineapple-Champagne Punch

- **1 quart pineapple sherbet**
- **1 quart unsweetened pineapple juice, chilled**
- **1 bottle (750 mL) dry champagne, chilled**
- **2 fresh or canned pineapple slices, each cut into 6 wedges**
- **Mint sprigs**

1. Process sherbet and pineapple juice in blender until smooth and frothy. Pour into punch bowl. Stir in champagne.

2. Float pineapple wedges in punch in groups of 3 or 4 to form flowers; garnish with mint sprigs. Serve immediately.   *Makes 20 (4-ounce) servings*

Hot Mulled Apple Cider

- **$1/2$ gallon apple cider**
- **$1/2$ cup packed light brown sugar**
- **1 $1/2$ teaspoons balsamic or cider vinegar**
- **1 teaspoon vanilla**
- **1 cinnamon stick**
- **6 whole cloves**
- **$1/2$ cup applejack or bourbon (optional)**

Combine all ingredients except applejack in large saucepan; bring to a boil. Reduce heat to low; simmer, uncovered, 10 minutes. Remove from heat; stir in applejack, if desired. Pour into punch bowl.   *Makes 16 servings*

43

Cranberry Sangría

- 1 bottle (750 mL) Beaujolais or dry red wine
- 1 cup cranberry juice cocktail
- 1 cup orange juice
- ½ cup cranberry-flavored liqueur (optional)
- 1 orange,* thinly sliced
- 1 lime,* thinly sliced

The orange and lime can be scored before slicing to add a special touch. To score, make a lengthwise groove in the fruit with a citrus stripper. Continue to make grooves ¼ to ½ inch apart until the entire fruit has been grooved.

1. Combine wine, cranberry juice cocktail, orange juice, liqueur, if desired, orange and lime slices in large glass pitcher. Chill 2 to 8 hours before serving.

2. Pour into glasses; add orange and/or lime slices from sangría to each glass.

Makes about 7 cups, 10 to 12 servings

Sparkling Sangría: Just before serving, tilt pitcher and slowly add 2 cups well-chilled sparkling water or club soda. Makes about 9 cups, or 12 to 15 servings.

Hot Mulled Pineapple Juice

- 6 cups DOLE® Pineapple Juice
- 1 apple, cored and cut into chunks
- ½ cup DOLE® Seedless Raisins
- ½ cup packed brown sugar
- Grated peel of 1 orange
- 2 cinnamon sticks, broken
- ½ teaspoon whole cloves

✦ Combine pineapple juice, apple chunks, raisins, brown sugar, peel, cinnamon sticks and cloves in saucepan. Simmer 5 minutes.

✦ Remove and discard spices before serving.

Makes 6 servings

44

Cranberry Sangría

Egg Cream

½ cup half-and-half

2 tablespoons lite chocolate syrup

2 cups unsweetened seltzer water or club soda, well chilled

Pour ¼ cup half-and-half into each of two tall glasses; stir 1 tablespoon chocolate syrup into each. Top off each glass with 1 cup seltzer.   *Makes 2 servings*

Hot Holiday Punch

4 cups apple cider

1 cup granulated sugar

½ cup packed brown sugar

1 cinnamon stick

12 whole cloves

2 cups Florida grapefruit juice

2 cups Florida orange juice

   Florida orange slices

   Maraschino cherry halves (optional)

   Whole cloves (optional)

Combine apple cider and sugars in large saucepan. Heat over medium heat, stirring until sugars dissolve. Add cinnamon stick and cloves. Bring to a boil over medium heat. Reduce heat to low; simmer 5 minutes. Add grapefruit and orange juices. Heat, but do not boil. Strain into heatproof punch bowl. Garnish with orange slices decorated with maraschino cherry halves and whole cloves. Serve in heatproof punch cups.

Makes 8 (8-ounce) servings

Favorite recipe from **Florida Department of Citrus**

46

Egg Cream

Strawberry Champagne Punch

2 packages (10 ounces each) frozen sliced strawberries in syrup, thawed
2 cans (5 1/2 ounces each) apricot or peach nectar
1/4 cup lemon juice
2 tablespoons honey
2 bottles (750 mL each) champagne or sparkling white wine, chilled
     Lemon slices, fresh strawberry halves and mint leaves, for garnish

1. Place strawberries with syrup in food processor; process until smooth.

2. Pour puréed strawberries into large punch bowl. Stir in apricot nectar, lemon juice and honey; blend well. Refrigerate until serving time.

3. To serve, stir champagne into strawberry mixture. Garnish as desired.

Makes 12 servings

Tip: To save time, thaw the strawberries in the refrigerator the day before using them.

Prep Time: 15 minutes

Celebration Punch

1 can (46 fluid ounces) **DEL MONTE®** Pineapple Juice, chilled
1 can (46 fluid ounces) apricot nectar, chilled
1 cup orange juice
1/4 cup fresh lime juice
2 tablespoons grenadine
1 cup rum (optional)
     Ice cubes

1. Combine all ingredients in punch bowl.

2. Garnish with pineapple wedges and lime slices, if desired.

Makes 16 (6-ounce) servings

48

Strawberry Champagne Punch

Hot Spiced Cider

2 quarts apple cider
²/₃ cup **KARO®** Light or Dark Corn Syrup
3 cinnamon sticks
¹/₂ teaspoon whole cloves
1 lemon, sliced
Cinnamon sticks and lemon slices (optional)

1. In medium saucepan combine cider, corn syrup, cinnamon sticks, cloves and lemon slices.

2. Bring to boil over medium-high heat. Reduce heat; simmer 15 minutes. Remove spices.

3. If desired, garnish each serving with a cinnamon stick and lemon slice.

Makes about 10 servings

50

Prep Time: 20 minutes

Peanutty Nog

1 cup skim milk
2 teaspoons creamy peanut butter
2 teaspoons granulated sugar
Pinch pumpkin pie spice

Add all ingredients to food processor or blender. Process until smooth and frothy. Serve immediately.

Makes 2 servings

Favorite recipe from **The Sugar Association, Inc.**

51

Hot Spiced Cider

Citrus Punch

Frozen Fruit Ice (recipe follows)

2 **cups orange juice**

2 **cups grapefruit juice**

3/4 **cup lime juice**

1/2 **cup light corn syrup**

1 **bottle (750 mL) ginger ale, white grape juice, Asti Spumante or sparkling wine**

Fresh mint sprigs for garnish

4 **oranges, sectioned**

1 **to 2 limes, cut into 1/8-inch slices**

1 **lemon, cut into 1/8-inch slices**

1 **pint strawberries, stemmed and halved**

1 **cup raspberries**

1. Prepare Frozen Fruit Ice.

2. Combine juices and corn syrup in 2-quart pitcher. Stir until corn syrup dissolves. (Stir in additional corn syrup to taste.) Refrigerate 2 hours or until cold. Stir in ginger ale just before serving.

3. Divide Frozen Fruit Ice between 8 (12-ounce) glasses or 10 wide-rimmed wine glasses. Fill glasses with punch. Garnish, if desired. Serve immediately.

Makes 8 to 10 servings (about 5 cups)

Frozen Fruit Ice: Spread oranges, limes, lemon, strawberries and raspberries on baking sheet. Freeze 4 hours or until firm.

Banana Nog

2 cups milk

1 large ripe banana, cut into pieces

$1/2$ cup sugar

1 tablespoon cornstarch

2 egg yolks

$2/3$ cup light rum

$1/4$ cup crème de cacao

1 teaspoon vanilla

2 cups half-and-half, chilled

Whipped cream

Unsweetened cocoa powder

6 miniature candy canes

Supplies

Red and/or green ribbon

1. Process milk and banana in blender or food processor until smooth. Mix sugar and cornstarch in medium saucepan; stir in milk mixture. Heat to simmering over medium heat, stirring occasionally.

2. Lightly beat egg yolks in small bowl; whisk about $1/2$ cup milk mixture into egg yolks. Whisk yolk mixture back into saucepan. Cook over medium heat, stirring constantly, until thick enough to coat the back of a spoon. Do not boil.

3. Remove from heat; stir in rum, crème de cacao and vanilla. Pour into large heatproof pitcher or bowl. Cover; refrigerate until chilled.

4. Just before serving, stir half-and-half into eggnog mixture. Serve in mugs or punch cups; garnish with dollops of whipped cream and sprinkles of cocoa. Tie pieces of ribbon around candy canes; use as stirrers.

Makes 6 servings (about 6 ounces each)

Roasted Chicken with Maple Glaze

- 1 broiler-fryer chicken (about 3 pounds)
- 1 small onion, cut into wedges
- 1 small orange, cut into wedges
- ¾ cup apple cider
- ¼ cup maple syrup
- ¾ teaspoon cornstarch
- ¼ teaspoon pumpkin pie spice

1. Preheat oven to 325°F. Remove giblets and neck from chicken; reserve for another use. Rinse chicken under cold water; pat dry with paper towels.

2. Place onion and orange wedges in cavity of chicken. Tie legs together with wet cotton string and place breast-side up on rack in shallow roasting pan coated with nonstick cooking spray. Insert meat thermometer into meaty part of thigh not touching bone.

3. Combine apple cider, maple syrup, cornstarch and pumpkin pie spice in small saucepan, stirring until cornstarch is dissolved. Bring to a boil over medium heat, stirring constantly; cook 1 minute. Brush apple cider mixture over chicken.

4. Bake chicken 1½ to 2 hours or until meat thermometer registers 180°F, basting frequently with remaining cider mixture.

5. Remove string from chicken; discard. Remove onion and orange wedges from chicken cavity; discard. Transfer chicken to serving platter. Let stand 10 minutes before carving.

Makes 6 servings

Roasted Chicken with Maple Glaze

Boiled Whole Lobster
with Burned Butter Sauce

- ½ cup (1 stick) butter
- 2 tablespoons chopped fresh parsley
- 1 tablespoon capers
- 1 tablespoon cider vinegar
- 2 live lobsters

1. Fill 8-quart stockpot with enough water to cover lobsters. Cover stockpot; bring water to a boil over high heat. Meanwhile, to make Burned Butter Sauce, melt butter in medium saucepan over medium heat. Cook and stir until butter turns dark chocolate brown. Remove from heat. Add parsley, capers and vinegar. Pour into 2 individual ramekins; set aside.

2. Holding each lobster by its back, submerge head first into boiling water. Cover and continue to heat. When water returns to a boil, cook lobsters for 10 to 18 minutes, depending on size.

3. Transfer to 2 large serving platters. Remove bands restraining claws. Cut through underside of shells with kitchen shears and loosen meat from shells. Provide nutcrackers and seafood forks. Serve lobsters with Burned Butter Sauce.

Makes 2 servings

Tip: Purchase live lobsters as close to time of cooking as possible. Store in refrigerator until ready to cook.

56

Boiled Whole Lobster with Burned Butter Sauce

Crown Roast of Pork with Peach Stuffing

1 (7- to 8-pound) crown roast of pork (12 to 16 ribs)
1 ½ cups water
1 cup FLEISCHMANN'S® Original Margarine, divided
1 (15-ounce) package seasoned bread cubes
1 cup chopped celery
2 medium onions, chopped
1 (16-ounce) can sliced peaches, drained and chopped, liquid reserved
½ cup seedless raisins

1. Place crown roast, bone tips up, on rack in shallow roasting pan. Make a ball of foil; press into cavity to hold open. Wrap bone tips in foil. Roast at 325°F, uncovered, for 2 hours; baste with pan drippings occasionally.

2. Heat water and ¾ cup margarine to a boil in large heavy pot; remove from heat. Add bread cubes, tossing lightly with a fork; set aside.

3. Cook and stir celery and onions in remaining margarine in large skillet over medium-high heat until tender, about 5 minutes.

4. Add celery mixture, peaches with liquid and raisins to bread cube mixture, tossing to mix well.

5. Remove foil from center of roast. Spoon stuffing lightly into cavity. Roast 30 to 45 minutes more or until meat thermometer registers 155°F (internal temperature will rise to 160°F upon standing). Cover stuffing with foil, if necessary, to prevent overbrowning. Bake any remaining stuffing in greased, covered casserole during last 30 minutes of roasting.

Makes 12 to 16 servings

Prep Time: 45 minutes
Cook Time: 2 hours 30 minutes
Total Time: 3 hours 15 minutes

58

59

Crown Roast of Pork with Peach Stuffing

Southwest Hopping John

1 ½ cups dried black-eyed peas
2 tablespoons olive oil
1 medium onion, chopped
4 cloves garlic, minced
2 medium red or green bell peppers, chopped
1 jalapeño pepper,* minced
1 teaspoon ground cumin
2 ½ cups canned chicken broth
1 cup uncooked brown basmati rice
¼ pound smoked ham, diced
4 medium tomatoes, seeded and chopped
½ cup minced fresh cilantro

Jalapeño peppers can sting and irritate the skin; wear rubber gloves when handling peppers and do not touch eyes. Wash hands after handling.

1. Rinse peas thoroughly in colander under cold running water. Place in large bowl; cover with 4 inches of water. Let stand at least 8 hours, then rinse and drain.

2. Transfer peas to medium saucepan; cover with water. Bring to a boil over high heat. Reduce heat to low; simmer, covered, 1 hour or until tender. Drain in colander; set aside.

3. Heat oil in Dutch oven over medium-high heat. Add onion and garlic; cook and stir 2 minutes. Add bell and jalapeño peppers; cook and stir 2 minutes. Stir in cumin; cook and stir 1 minute.

4. Stir in chicken broth, rice and ham. Bring to a boil over high heat. Reduce heat to low; simmer, covered, 35 minutes.

5. Add peas; simmer 10 minutes or until liquid is absorbed. Stir tomatoes and cilantro into rice mixture just before serving. Garnish as desired. *Makes 6 servings*

Southwest Hopping John

Roast Chicken & Kiwifruit with Raspberry Glaze

- 2 chickens, quartered (3 1/2 to 4 pounds each)
- 1 teaspoon salt
- 1/4 teaspoon black pepper
- 2 tablespoons butter or margarine, melted
- Raspberry Glaze (recipe follows)
- 2 kiwifruit, peeled and sliced

Preheat oven to 400°F. Sprinkle chicken with salt and pepper. Place, skin side up, in single layer in large, shallow pan; brush with butter. Roast, basting frequently with butter, about 45 minutes or until chicken is tender and juices run clear. Drain off fat. While chicken is roasting, prepare Raspberry Glaze. Spoon glaze over chicken; top with kiwifruit slices. Spoon glaze from bottom of pan over chicken and kiwifruit. Bake about 5 minutes, basting frequently with pan juices, or until kiwifruit and chicken are well glazed.

Makes 8 servings

Raspberry Glaze: Combine 1 cup seedless raspberry preserves, 1/2 cup white port wine and grated peel of 1 lemon in small saucepan. Cook over low heat about 5 minutes or until slightly thickened.

Favorite recipe from **Delmarva Poultry Industry, Inc.**

Tips to share

Port wine is a fortified wine that has brandy or other alcohol added to it for the purpose of increasing its alcoholic content. Wine can be omitted in most recipes that call for it, although adjustments in the amount of liquid may be required.

62

Roast Chicken & Kiwifruit with Raspberry Glaze

Mustard Crusted Rib Roast

1 (3-rib) beef rib roast, trimmed* (6 to 7 pounds)

3 tablespoons Dijon mustard

1 tablespoon plus 1 1/2 teaspoons chopped fresh tarragon *or* 1 1/2 teaspoons dried tarragon leaves

3 cloves garlic, minced

1/4 cup dry red wine

1/3 cup finely chopped shallots (about 2 shallots)

1 tablespoon all-purpose flour

1 cup beef broth

Mashed potatoes (optional)

Fresh tarragon sprigs for garnish

Ask meat retailer to remove chine bone for easier carving. Trim fat to 1/4-inch thickness.

1. Preheat oven to 450°F. Place roast, bone-side-down, in shallow roasting pan. Combine mustard, chopped tarragon and garlic in small bowl; spread over all surfaces of roast, except bottom. Insert meat thermometer into thickest part of roast, not touching bone or fat. Roast 10 minutes.

2. *Reduce oven temperature* to 350°F. Roast 2 1/2 to 3 hours for medium or until internal temperature reaches 145°F when tested with meat thermometer inserted into thickest part of roast, without touching bone.

3. Transfer roast to cutting board; cover with foil. Let stand 10 to 15 minutes before carving. Internal temperature will continue to rise 5° to 10°F during stand time.

4. To make gravy, pour fat from roasting pan, reserving 1 tablespoon in medium saucepan. Add wine to roasting pan; place over 2 burners. Cook over medium heat 2 minutes or until slightly thickened, stirring to scrape up browned bits; reserve.

5. Add shallots to reserved drippings in saucepan; cook and stir over medium heat 4 minutes or until softened. Add flour; cook and stir 1 minute. Add broth and reserved wine mixture; cook 5 minutes or until sauce thickens, stirring occasionally. Pour through strainer into gravy boat, pressing with back of spoon on shallots; discard solids.

6. Carve roast into 1/2-inch-thick slices. Serve with gravy and mashed potatoes, if desired. Garnish, if desired.

Makes 6 to 8 servings

Mustard Crusted Rib Roast

Flounder Stuffed with Crabmeat Imperial

2 whole baby flounder (about 1 to 1 1/4 pounds each)*

1 cup crabmeat, picked over for shell and cartilage

1/4 cup mayonnaise

2 tablespoons minced green bell pepper

1 teaspoon Worcestershire sauce

1 teaspoon prepared mustard

1 teaspoon chopped pimiento

Dash salt and black pepper

2 tablespoons seasoned bread crumbs

1 tablespoon melted butter

Flat fish, such as flounder, are generally sold as fillets. Whole flat fish may need to be special ordered from your seafood retailer. Flounder should be gutted and scaled with head and tail left on.

1. Preheat oven to 375°F.

2. Rinse flounder; pat dry with paper towels. Place fish on greased baking sheet with head side up. Cut slit down backbone of each fish, which is in the center of the top of the fish, using sharp utility knife.

3. Starting on 1 side of each fish, insert knife horizontally into slit. Begin cutting, about 1 inch from head, between flesh and bone, stopping just before tail to form pocket. Cut another pocket on opposite side of fish.

4. To make stuffing, combine crabmeat, mayonnaise, bell pepper, Worcestershire, mustard, pimiento, salt and black pepper in small bowl. Spoon mixture evenly into prepared fish pockets.

5. Sprinkle fish with bread crumbs and drizzle with butter. Bake 25 minutes or until fish flakes easily when tested with fork. Garnish, if desired.   *Makes 2 servings*

67

Flounder Stuffed with Crabmeat Imperial

Roast Pork with Tart Cherries

1 boneless rolled pork roast (3 $\frac{1}{2}$ to 4 pounds)

3 teaspoons bottled grated horseradish, divided

1 teaspoon ground coriander

$\frac{1}{2}$ teaspoon black pepper

1 can (16 ounces) pitted tart cherries, undrained

$\frac{1}{2}$ cup chicken broth

$\frac{1}{3}$ cup Madeira wine or dry sherry

1 tablespoon brown sugar

1 tablespoon Dijon mustard

$\frac{1}{8}$ teaspoon ground cloves

4 teaspoons grated orange peel

Orange peel twist (optional)

1. Preheat oven to 400°F. Place pork on meat rack in shallow roasting pan. Insert meat thermometer into thickest part of roast.

2. Combine 2 teaspoons horseradish, coriander and pepper in small bowl. Rub over pork. Roast pork 10 minutes; remove from oven. *Reduce oven temperature to 350°F.*

3. Add cherries with juice and broth to pan. Cover pan loosely with foil. Roast about 1 hour 30 minutes, basting every 20 minutes, or until internal temperature of roast reaches 165°F when tested with meat thermometer inserted into the thickest part of roast. (Cook, uncovered, during last 20 minutes).

4. Transfer pork to cutting board; cover with foil. Let stand 10 to 15 minutes before carving. Internal temperature will continue to rise 5° to 10°F during stand time.

5. Meanwhile, remove meat rack from roasting pan. Pour contents of pan through strainer into small saucepan, reserving cherries. Stir wine, sugar, mustard, remaining 1 teaspoon horseradish, cloves and grated orange peel into saucepan. Bring to a boil over medium-high heat. Boil 10 minutes or until sauce is thickened. Stir in reserved cherries.

6. Carve pork into thin slices; place on serving platter. Pour some cherry sauce around pork. Serve with remaining cherry sauce. Garnish with orange peel twist, if desired.

Makes 8 servings

Roast Pork with Tart Cherries

Steamed Maryland Crabs

2 cups water or beer
2 cups cider vinegar or white vinegar
2 dozen live Maryland blue crabs
$^1/_2$ pound seafood seasoning
$^1/_2$ pound salt

1. Place water and vinegar in 10-gallon stockpot. Place steaming rack in bottom of pot. Place half of crabs on rack. Mix seafood seasoning with salt; sprinkle half over crabs.

2. Repeat layering with remaining crabs and seasoning mixture.

3. Cover pot. Cook over high heat until liquid begins to steam. Steam about 25 minutes or until crabs turn red and meat is white. Remove crabs to large serving platter using tongs.

4. To serve, cover table with disposable paper cloth.

5. To pick crabs, place crab on its back. With thumb or knife point, pry off "apron" flap (the "pull tab" looking shell in the center) and discard.

6. Lift off top shell and discard.

7. Break off toothed claws and set aside. With knife edge, scrape off 3 areas of lungs and debris over hard semi-transparent membrane covering edible crabmeat.

8. Hold crab at each side; break apart at center. Discard legs. Remove membrane cover with knife, exposing large chunks of meat; remove with fingers or knife.

9. Crack claws with mallet or knife handle to expose meat.   *Makes 4 servings*

Steamed Maryland Crabs

71

Roast Turkey Breast with Sausage and Apple Stuffing

8 ounces bulk pork sausage

1 medium apple, cored, peeled and finely chopped

1 shallot or small onion, peeled and finely chopped

1 celery stalk, finely chopped

1/4 cup chopped hazelnuts

1/2 teaspoon rubbed sage, divided

1/2 teaspoon salt, divided

1/2 teaspoon black pepper, divided

1 tablespoon butter

1 turkey breast (4 1/2 to 5 pounds), thawed if frozen

4 to 6 fresh sage leaves (optional)

1 cup chicken broth

1. Preheat oven to 325°F. Crumble pork sausage into large skillet. Add apple, shallot and celery. Cook and stir until sausage is cooked through and apple and vegetables are tender. Stir in hazelnuts, 1/4 teaspoon sage, 1/4 teaspoon salt and 1/4 teaspoon pepper.

2. Mash butter with remaining 1/4 teaspoon each sage, salt and pepper. Spread over turkey breast skin. If desired, ease skin over turkey breast. Arrange sage leaves under skin. Spoon sausage stuffing into turkey cavity. Close cavity with metal skewers. Place turkey, skin side down on rack in shallow roasting pan. Pour broth into pan.

3. Roast turkey 45 minutes. Remove turkey from oven, turn skin side up. Baste with broth. Return to oven and roast 1 hour, or until meat thermometer registers 170°F. Remove from oven. Let turkey rest 10 minutes before slicing.   *Makes 6 servings*

Roast Turkey Breast with Sausage
and Apple Stuffing

Glazed Roast Lamb with Rhubarb Salsa

3 tablespoons honey

2 tablespoons red wine vinegar

1 teaspoon garlic salt

1/4 teaspoon ground black pepper

1 American leg of lamb (4 to 6 pounds), boned and rolled

Rhubarb Salsa (recipe follows)

Combine honey, vinegar, garlic salt and pepper. Place lamb on rack in roasting pan; brush with honey mixture. Roast in 325°F oven 2 to 4 hours or until desired doneness (160°F for medium), brushing occasionally with honey mixture.

Meanwhile prepare Rhubarb Salsa. Serve salsa at room temperature with lamb.

Makes 12 servings

Rhubarb Salsa

1 cup chopped onion

2/3 cup dark or golden raisins

1/2 cup honey

2 tablespoons red wine vinegar

3 to 4 teaspoons chopped jalapeño pepper*

2 cloves garlic, minced

1/2 teaspoon ground cardamom

6 cups (1 1/2 pounds) fresh or frozen sliced rhubarb

Jalapeño peppers can sting and irritate the skin. Wear rubber gloves when handling and do not touch eyes.

In large saucepan, combine onion, raisins, honey, vinegar, jalapeño pepper, garlic and cardamom. Stir in rhubarb. Bring to a boil; reduce heat and simmer, covered, 10 minutes, stirring as little as possible. Uncover; simmer 5 minutes to reduce liquid slightly. Stir only if necessary to prevent scorching. Set aside. Refrigerate any leftovers.

Favorite recipe from **American Lamb Council**

74

Glazed Roast Lamb with Rhubarb Salsa

Roast Garlic Chicken

1 whole broiler-fryer chicken (about 3 to 4 pounds)
2 tablespoons lemon juice
1 1/2 teaspoons LAWRY'S® Garlic Powder With Parsley
2 teaspoons LAWRY'S® Seasoned Salt

Sprinkle chicken with lemon juice, Garlic Powder With Parsley and Seasoned Salt over outside and inside cavity of chicken. Spray 13×9×2-inch baking dish and roasting rack with nonstick cooking spray. Place chicken, breast side up, on roasting rack. Roast in 400°F oven 70 minutes, or until chicken is thoroughly cooked. Let stand 10 minutes before carving. *Makes 6 servings*

Tip: Loosely 'crunch up' some foil in the dish around the chicken to keep grease from splattering in the oven.

Prep Time: 10 minutes ✦ Cook Time: 70 minutes

Cranberry-Onion Pork Roast

1 boneless pork loin roast (about 2 pounds)
1 can (16 ounces) whole cranberry sauce
1 package (1 ounce) dry onion soup mix

Season roast with salt and pepper; place over indirect heat on grill; stir together cranberry sauce and onion soup mix and heat, covered, in microwave until hot, about 1 minute. Baste roast with cranberry mixture every 10 minutes until roast is done (internal temperature with a meat thermometer is 155° to 160°F), about 30 to 45 minutes; let roast rest about 5 to 8 minutes before slicing to serve. Heat any leftover basting mixture to boiling; stir and boil for 5 minutes. Serve alongside roast. *Makes 4 to 6 servings*

Favorite recipe from **National Pork Board**

Roast Garlic Chicken

Herb Roasted Turkey with Citrus Glaze

1 (15-pound) fresh or thawed frozen Whole Turkey

3 large lemons

2 large limes

1 ½ teaspoons salt

½ teaspoon coarsely ground black pepper

¼ cup dry white wine*

¼ cup packed brown sugar

1 bunch *each* fresh sage and marjoram

Olive or vegetable oil

Alcohol-free wine can be substituted for the dry white wine.

1. Remove giblets and neck from turkey; reserve for gravy. Rinse turkey with cold running water; drain well. Blot dry with paper towels.

2. Peel lemons and limes to make rose garnishes (recipe follows); reserve.

3. Squeeze enough juice from lemons and limes to equal 2 tablespoons each. Cut remaining lemons and lime in half; place in turkey cavity. Sprinkle salt in cavity.

4. In small bowl, combine wine, brown sugar and citrus juices; reserve for glaze.

5. Gently loosen skin from turkey breast without totally detaching skin and carefully place 1 tablespoon each sage and marjoram under skin. Replace skin.

6. Fold neck skin and fasten to back with 1 or 2 skewers. Fold wings under back of turkey. Return legs to tucked position.

7. Preheat oven to 325°F. Place turkey, breast side up, on rack in large shallow (about 2½-inches-deep) roasting pan. Rub turkey with salt, pepper and 2 to 3 tablespoons oil. Insert oven-safe meat thermometer into thickest part of thigh, being careful pointed end of thermometer does not touch bone.

8. Roast turkey 3 hours and 45 minutes. During last hour of roasting time, baste with pan drippings. During last 30 minutes, baste with citrus glaze. Loosely cover with lightweight foil to prevent excessive browning. Continue to roast until thermometer registers 180°F in thigh.

9. Remove turkey from oven and allow to rest 15 to 20 minutes before carving.

10. Place on warm large platter; garnish with remaining fresh herbs and lemon and lime roses.

Makes 22 servings

Rose Garnishes: With small sharp knife or vegetable peeler, cut continuous thin 1-inch strip of reserved lemon or lime peel. Avoid cutting into white pith. Roll tightly, skin inside out, and secure with toothpicks. Reserve in bowl filled with ice water until time of service.

Favorite recipe from **National Turkey Federation**

Steamed Bucket of Clams

    18 to 24 hard-shell clams
     1 gallon cold water
    1/3 cup cornmeal
    1/3 cup salt
        Juice of 1 SUNKIST® lemon
     2 tablespoons olive or vegetable oil
        Grated peel of 1/2 SUNKIST® lemon
     2 tablespoons chopped parsley
        SUNKIST® lemon wedges

Scrub clams well. To purge clams, combine water, cornmeal and salt. Add clams; soak for 2 hours. Rinse well. In 10-inch skillet, arrange clams in single layer; drizzle with lemon juice and oil. Bring liquid to a boil over medium-high heat; cover tightly and cook 5 minutes. Do not lift lid of skillet during this cooking time. (If most clams have not opened, cook, covered, 1 to 2 minutes longer.) Remove clams to serving bowl; discard any unopened clams. Stir lemon peel and parsley into clam juice in skillet. Pour over clams. Serve with lemon wedges.

Makes 2 to 4 servings

Sweet Potatoes with Brandy and Raisins

1/2 cup seedless raisins

1/4 cup brandy

4 medium sweet potatoes, boiled until just tender then peeled and sliced into 1/4-inch slices

2/3 cup packed brown sugar

1/4 cup **FLEISCHMANN'S®** Original Margarine

2 tablespoons water

1/4 teaspoon ground cinnamon

1. Mix raisins and brandy in small bowl; let stand 20 minutes. Drain raisins.

2. Layer sweet potatoes in 9×9×2-inch baking pan; top with raisins.

3. Mix brown sugar, margarine, water and cinnamon in small saucepan; heat to a boil. Pour over sweet potatoes.

4. Bake in preheated 350°F oven for 40 minutes, basting with pan juices occasionally.

Makes 4 to 6 servings

Preparation Time: 20 minutes ✦ *Cook Time:* 40 minutes ✦ *Total Time:* 1 hour

Sweet Potatoes with Brandy and Raisins

Potato Pancakes with Apple-Cherry Chutney

Apple-Cherry Chutney (recipe follows)
1 pound baking potatoes (about 2 medium)
$^1/_2$ small onion
3 egg whites
2 tablespoons all-purpose flour
$^1/_2$ teaspoon salt
$^1/_4$ teaspoon black pepper
4 teaspoons vegetable oil, divided

1. Prepare Apple-Cherry Chutney; set aside.

2. Wash and scrub potatoes; cut into chunks. Combine potatoes, onion, egg whites, flour, salt and pepper in food processor or blender; process until almost smooth (mixture will appear grainy).

3. Heat large nonstick skillet 1 minute over medium heat. Add 1 teaspoon oil. Spoon $^1/_3$ cup batter per pancake into skillet. Cook 3 pancakes at a time, 3 minutes per side or until golden brown. Repeat with remaining batter, adding 1 teaspoon oil with each batch. Serve with Apple-Cherry Chutney. Garnish, if desired.   *Makes 6 servings*

Apple-Cherry Chutney

1 cup chunky applesauce
$^1/_2$ cup canned tart cherries, drained
2 tablespoons brown sugar
1 teaspoon lemon juice
$^1/_2$ teaspoon ground cinnamon
$^1/_8$ teaspoon ground nutmeg

Combine all ingredients in small saucepan; bring to a boil. Reduce heat; simmer 5 minutes. Serve warm.   *Makes 1 $^1/_2$ cups*

Potato Pancakes with Apple-Cherry Chutney

Orange-Glazed Carrots

- 1 pound fresh baby carrots
- 1/3 cup orange marmalade
- 2 tablespoons butter
- 2 teaspoons Dijon mustard
- 1/2 teaspoon grated fresh ginger

Heat 1 inch lightly salted water in 2-quart saucepan over high heat to a boil; add carrots. Return to a boil. Reduce heat to low. Cover and simmer 10 to 12 minutes or until crisp-tender. Drain well; return carrots to pan. Stir in marmalade, butter, mustard and ginger. Simmer uncovered over medium heat 3 minutes or until carrots are glazed, stirring occasionally.*

Makes 6 servings

At this point, carrots may be transferred to a microwavable casserole dish with lid. Cover and refrigerate up to 8 hours before serving. To reheat, microwave at HIGH (100% power) 4 to 5 minutes or until hot.

Applesauce Cranberry Mold

- 2 envelopes unflavored gelatin
- 1/2 cup orange or cranberry juice
- 1/2 cup boiling water
- 1 can or jar (16 ounces) whole-berry cranberry sauce
- 1 cup applesauce
- 1 apple, cored and cut up
- 1 cup diced celery
- 1/2 cup chopped walnuts
- 1 orange, peeled and diced
- 2 tablespoons grated orange peel

Soften gelatin in juice. Add boiling water and stir to dissolve; cool. Mix all other ingredients; add to gelatin mixture. Pour into greased 2-quart mold and refrigerate several hours.

Makes 6 to 8 servings

Favorite recipe from **New York Apple Association, Inc.**

Orange-Glazed Carrots

Two-Toned Stuffed Potatoes

3 large baking potatoes (12 ounces each)
2 large sweet potatoes (12 ounces each), dark flesh preferred
3 slices thick-cut bacon, cut in half crosswise on a diagonal
2 cups coarsely chopped onion
2/3 cup buttermilk
1/4 cup (1/2 stick) butter, cut in small pieces
3/4 teaspoon salt, divided

1. Preheat oven to 450°F. Pierce potatoes with fork in several places. Bake directly on oven rack 45 minutes or until fork-tender. *Reduce oven to 350°F.*

2. Meanwhile, cook bacon 6 to 8 minutes in medium skillet over medium-high heat, until crisp. Remove from heat; transfer bacon with slotted spoon to paper towels and set aside.

3. Add onions to bacon fat in skillet; cook about 12 minutes over medium-high heat, until golden brown; reserve. Remove skillet from heat; add buttermilk, scraping up any browned bits from bottom of pan. Add butter, swirling to melt.

4. Slice baking potatoes lengthwise with serrated knife; scoop out flesh into large bowl. Reserve skins. Add about 3/4 cup of buttermilk mixture, 1/2 teaspoon salt and about 1/2 cup of cooked onion. Mash with potato masher until smooth.

5. Slice sweet potatoes lengthwise with serrated knife; scoop out flesh into medium bowl. Discard skins. Add remaining buttermilk mixture, 1/4 teaspoon salt and remaining cooked onion. Mash with potato masher until smooth.

6. Fill half of each reserved potato skin horizontally, vertically or diagonally with baked potato mixture, using spoon; fill other half with sweet-potato mixture. Top each stuffed potato half with half slice of bacon.

7. Transfer stuffed potatoes to sheet pan; cook 15 minutes until heated through.

Makes 6 servings

Tip: Stuffed potatoes can be made weeks in advance and frozen. Reheat frozen potatoes in a 350°F oven for 75 to 90 minutes. If made ahead and refrigerated for a few days, reheat in a 350°F oven for 25 minutes.

Two-Toned Stuffed Potatoes

Cranberry Salad

2 cups cranberries

I cup water

I cup **EQUAL® SPOONFUL***

I small package cranberry or cherry sugar-free gelatin

I cup boiling water

I cup diced celery

I can (**7 1/4 ounces**) crushed pineapple, in juice

1/2 cup chopped walnuts

May substitute 24 packets EQUAL® sweetener.

✦ Bring cranberries and I cup water to a boil. Remove from heat when cranberries have popped open. Add Equal® and stir. Set aside to cool.

✦ Dissolve gelatin with I cup boiling water. Add cranberry sauce; mix thoroughly. Add celery, pineapple and walnuts. Pour into mold or bowl. Place in refrigerator until set.   *Makes 8 servings*

Wild Rice Apple Side Dish

I cup uncooked wild rice

3 1/2 cups chicken broth

1/2 teaspoon ground nutmeg

I cup dried apple slices

I cup chopped onion

I jar (**4.5 ounces**) sliced mushrooms, drained

1/2 cup thinly sliced celery

In large saucepan, simmer wild rice, broth and nutmeg 20 minutes. Add remaining ingredients; cover and simmer 20 to 30 minutes, stirring occasionally, until wild rice reaches desired doneness.   *Makes 6 servings*

Favorite recipe from **Minnesota Cultivated Wild Rice Council**

Cranberry Salad

Mashed Sweet Potatoes & Parsnips

2 large sweet potatoes (about 1 ¼ pounds), peeled and cut into 1-inch pieces

2 medium parsnips (about ½ pound), peeled and cut into ½-inch slices

¼ cup evaporated skimmed milk

1 ½ tablespoons butter or margarine

½ teaspoon salt

⅛ teaspoon ground nutmeg

¼ cup chopped chives or green onion tops

1. Combine sweet potatoes and parsnips in large saucepan. Cover with cold water and bring to a boil over high heat. Reduce heat; simmer uncovered 15 minutes or until vegetables are tender.

2. Drain vegetables; return to pan. Add milk, butter, salt and nutmeg. Mash potato mixture over low heat to desired consistency. Stir in chives.   *Makes 6 servings*

 Tips to share

Parsnips are good for soups, stews and vegetable side dishes. They pair well with herbs, such as rosemary, chives, thyme or tarragon. Plus their sweetness is enhanced by brown sugar, apples, orange zest and spices like cinnamon, ginger or nutmeg.

Mashed Sweet Potatoes & Parsnips

Baked Spiced Squash

2 boxes (10 ounces each) **BIRDS EYE®** frozen Cooked Winter Squash, thawed
2 egg whites, lightly beaten
1/4 cup brown sugar
2 teaspoons butter or margarine, melted
1 teaspoon ground cinnamon
1/2 cup herbed croutons, coarsely crushed

✦ Preheat oven to 400°F. Combine squash, egg whites, sugar, butter and cinnamon; mix well.

✦ Pour into 1-quart baking dish sprayed with nonstick cooking spray.

✦ Bake 20 to 25 minutes or until center is set.

✦ Remove from oven; sprinkle crushed croutons on top. Bake 5 to 7 minutes longer or until croutons are browned. *Makes 6 to 8 servings*

Prep Time: 5 minutes ✦ Cook Time: 25 to 35 minutes

92

Savory Apple Roast

2 baking apples
2 sweet potatoes
2 Vidalia onions
1 tablespoon olive oil
2 teaspoons chopped garlic
1 tablespoon balsamic vinegar

Preheat oven to 450°F. Line roasting pan with aluminum foil. Core and cut apples into quarters. Cut sweet potatoes into 6 to 8 large pieces. Cut onions into small wedges. Combine apples, vegetables, olive oil and garlic. Roast in prepared pan 40 to 45 minutes or until sweet potatoes are tender. Sprinkle with balsamic vinegar before serving. Serve hot or cold. *Makes 6 servings*

Preparation Time: 10 minutes ✦ Roasting Time: 40 to 45 minutes

Favorite recipe from **New York Apple Association, Inc.**

Baked Spiced Squash

93

Success Waldorf Dressing

1 box SUCCESS® Long Grain & Wild Rice Mix
3 strips bacon
1/2 cup chopped celery
1 medium red apple, chopped
1 medium green apple, chopped
1/2 cup chopped walnuts
1/2 cup raisins
2 tablespoons honey
2 tablespoons lemon juice

Prepare rice mix according to package directions.

Meanwhile, cook bacon in skillet until crisp. Remove bacon and crumble. Cook and stir celery in same skillet until tender. Add remaining ingredients. Fold in cooked rice. Top with crumbled bacon. *Makes 4 to 6 servings*

Cinnamon Apple Sweet Potatoes

4 medium sweet potatoes
1 1/2 cups finely chopped apples
1/2 cup orange juice
1/4 cup sugar
1 1/2 teaspoons cornstarch
1/2 teaspoon ground cinnamon
1/2 teaspoon grated orange peel

Microwave Directions
Prick potatoes with fork. Place on paper towels and microwave on HIGH (100%) 10 to 13 minutes or until tender, turning halfway through cooking. Set aside. In microwavable bowl, combine remaining ingredients. Cover and cook on HIGH 3 minutes; stir. Cook uncovered on HIGH 1 1/2 to 2 1/2 minutes or until sauce is thickened. Slit sweet potatoes and spoon sauce over each. *Makes 4 servings*

Tip: Sauce can be made ahead and reheated.

Favorite recipe from **The Sugar Association, Inc.**

Success Waldorf Dressing

Tomato Scalloped Potatoes

1 can (14 1/2 ounces) **DEL MONTE®** Diced Tomatoes
1 pound red potatoes, thinly sliced
1 medium onion, chopped
1/2 cup whipping cream
1 cup (4 ounces) shredded Swiss cheese
3 tablespoons grated Parmesan cheese

1. Preheat oven to 350°F.

2. Drain tomatoes, reserving liquid; pour liquid into measuring cup. Add water to measure 1 cup.

3. Add reserved liquid, potatoes and onion to large skillet; cover. Cook 10 minutes or until tender.

4. Place potato mixture in 1-quart baking dish; top with tomatoes and cream. Sprinkle with cheeses.

5. Bake 20 minutes or until hot and bubbly. Sprinkle with chopped parsley, if desired.

Makes 6 servings

Prep Time: 8 minutes ✦ Cook Time: 30 minutes

Tips to share

To scallop refers to the technique of preparing a food by slicing or cutting it into small pieces and layering it in a casserole with a creamy sauce. Scalloped potatoes and scalloped oysters are probably the best known dishes prepared this way.

96

Maple-Glazed Squash

1 large acorn squash, seeded and cut into quarters

Butter-flavored vegetable cooking spray

1 large tart cooking apple, unpeeled, cored and sliced

$1/4$ cup raisins

$1/4$ cup chopped walnuts

Maple-Flavored Syrup

1 cup apple juice

$2 1/2$ teaspoons cornstarch

1 tablespoon stick butter or margarine

$1/4$ cup **EQUAL® SPOONFUL***

1 teaspoon maple flavoring

1 teaspoon vanilla

May substitute 6 packets EQUAL® sweetener.

1. Place squash, cut sides up, in baking pan; add $1/2$ cup hot water to pan. Bake, covered, in preheated 400°F oven 30 to 40 minutes or until squash is tender.

2. Meanwhile, spray medium skillet with nonstick cooking spray; heat over medium heat until hot. Add apple, raisins and walnuts; cook over medium heat about 5 minutes or until apple slices are tender.

3. For Maple-Flavored Syrup, combine apple juice and cornstarch in small saucepan. Cook and stir until thickened and bubbly. Cook and stir 2 minutes more. Remove from heat; stir in butter, Equal®, maple flavoring and vanilla.

4. Add Maple-Flavored Syrup to apple mixture; cook until heated through, 2 to 3 minutes.

5. Place squash wedges on serving platter; spoon apple mixture over squash.

Makes 4 servings

Sage Buns

1 ½ cups milk

2 tablespoons shortening

3 to 4 cups all-purpose flour, divided

2 tablespoons sugar

1 package active dry yeast

2 teaspoons rubbed sage

1 teaspoon salt

1 tablespoon olive oil (optional)

1. Heat milk and shortening in small saucepan over medium heat, stirring constantly, until shortening is melted and temperature reaches 120° to 130°F. Remove from heat.

2. Combine 2 cups flour, sugar, yeast, sage and salt in large bowl. Add milk mixture; beat vigorously 2 minutes. Add remaining flour, ¼ cup at a time, until dough begins to pull away from sides of bowl.

3. Turn out dough onto floured work surface; flatten slightly. Knead 10 minutes or until dough is smooth and elastic, adding flour if necessary to prevent sticking.

4. Shape dough into ball. Place in large lightly oiled bowl; turn dough over once to oil surface. Cover with towel; let rise in warm place 1 hour or until doubled in bulk. Grease 13×9-inch pan; set aside.

5. Turn out dough onto lightly oiled surface. Divide into 24 equal pieces. Form each piece into ball. Place evenly spaced in prepared pan. Cover with towel; let rise 45 minutes.

6. Preheat oven to 375°F. Bake 15 to 20 minutes or until golden brown. Immediately remove bread from pan and cool on wire rack. Brush tops of rolls with olive oil for soft shiny tops, if desired.

Makes 24 rolls

Sage Buns

Cherry Buttermilk Loops

⅓ cup chopped dried cherries

½ cup water

Dough

  ½ cup buttermilk

  ¼ cup soaking liquid from cherries

  1 egg

  3 tablespoons butter, softened

  1 teaspoon salt

  3 cups bread flour

  ¼ cup sugar

  2 teaspoons active dry yeast

Topping

  ¼ cup cherry preserves, large cherry pieces chopped

1 ⅓ cups powdered sugar

  3 tablespoons buttermilk

¼ cup sliced almonds, toasted*

To toast almonds, spread in single layer on baking sheet. Bake in preheated 350°F oven 8 to 10 minutes or until golden brown, stirring frequently.

Bread Machine Directions

1. Place cherries and water in small microwavable bowl; cover. Microwave on HIGH (100% power) 30 seconds; let stand 5 minutes. Drain cherries, reserving ¼ cup soaking liquid for dough.

2. Measuring carefully, place all dough ingredients in bread machine pan in order specified by owner's manual, adding cherries with flour. Program dough cycle; press start. Lightly grease 2 baking sheets; set aside.

3. When cycle is complete, punch down dough; remove to lightly floured surface. If necessary, knead in additional bread flour to make dough easy to handle. Divide dough into 16 equal pieces. Gently roll and stretch each piece into 7-inch-long rope.

continued on page 102

100

Cherry Buttermilk Loops

Cherry Buttermilk Loops, *continued*

Shape each rope into half-figure-eight loop; place on prepared baking sheets. Cover with clean towel; let rise in warm, draft-free place 45 minutes or until doubled in size.

4. Preheat oven to 375°F. Bake 12 to 15 minutes or until golden brown. Meanwhile, heat preserves in small saucepan over low heat just until slightly warmed and softened, but not melted. Remove rolls from oven. Immediately brush entire surfaces generously with warm preserves. Remove from baking sheets; cool on wire racks.

5. Combine powdered sugar and buttermilk in small bowl, stirring until smooth. Place waxed paper under wire racks. Drizzle buttermilk icing over tops of rolls. Sprinkle with almonds. *Makes 16 rolls*

Whole Wheat Popovers

1 ¼ cups whole wheat pastry flour*
1 ¼ cups milk
3 eggs
2 tablespoons melted butter
¼ teaspoon salt
1 tablespoon cold butter, cut into 6 pieces

Whole wheat pastry flour is available at natural food stores and some supermarkets. Half white flour mixed with half whole wheat may be substituted.

1. Position rack in lower third of oven. Preheat oven to 400°F. Spray popover pan with nonstick cooking spray. (If popover pan is not available, jumbo muffin tin or custard cups may be used.)

2. Place flour, milk, eggs, melted butter and salt in food processor or blender. Process until batter is smooth and consistency of heavy cream. (Batter may also be blended in large bowl with electric mixer.) Meanwhile, place popover pan in oven for 2 minutes to preheat. Immediately place one piece of cold butter in each popover cup and return to oven 1 minute until butter melts.

3. Fill each cup halfway with batter. Bake 20 minutes. *Do not open oven or popovers may fall. Reduce oven temperature to 300°F.* Bake 20 minutes more. Remove from cups; cool slightly on wire rack. Serve warm. *Makes 6 popovers*

102

Whole Wheat Popovers

Sour Cream Coffeecake with Chocolate and Walnuts

¾ cup (1 ½ sticks) butter, softened

1 ½ cups packed light brown sugar

3 eggs

2 teaspoons vanilla

3 cups all-purpose flour

2 teaspoons baking powder

2 teaspoons ground cinnamon

1 ½ teaspoons baking soda

½ teaspoon ground nutmeg

¼ teaspoon salt

1 ½ cups sour cream

½ cup semisweet chocolate chips

½ cup chopped walnuts

Powdered sugar

1. Preheat oven to 350°F. Grease and flour 12-cup Bundt pan or 10-inch tube pan. Beat butter in large bowl with electric mixer on medium speed until creamy. Add brown sugar; beat until light and fluffy. Beat in eggs and vanilla until well blended. Combine flour, baking powder, cinnamon, baking soda, nutmeg and salt in large bowl; add to butter mixture on low speed alternately with sour cream, beginning and ending with flour mixture until well blended. Stir in chocolate chips and walnuts. Spoon into prepared pan.

2. Bake 45 to 50 minutes until toothpick inserted near center comes out clean. Cool in pan 15 minutes. Remove from pan to wire rack; cool completely. Store tightly covered at room temperature. Sprinkle with powdered sugar before serving.

Makes one 10-inch coffeecake

Sour Cream Coffeecake with Chocolate and Walnuts

Apple Crumb Coffeecake

2 1/4 cups all-purpose flour, divided

1/2 cup sugar

1 envelope FLEISCHMANN'S® RapidRise™ Yeast

1/2 teaspoon salt

1/4 cup water

1/4 cup milk

1/3 cup butter or margarine

2 large eggs

2 cooking apples, cored and sliced

Crumb Topping (recipe follows)

In large bowl, combine 1 cup flour, sugar, undissolved yeast and salt. Heat water, milk and butter until very warm (120° to 130°F). Gradually add to dry ingredients. Beat 2 minutes at medium speed of electric mixer, scraping bowl occasionally. Add eggs and 1/2 cup flour. Beat 2 minutes at high speed, scraping bowl occasionally. Stir in remaining 3/4 cup flour to make stiff batter. Spread evenly in greased 9-inch square pan. Arrange apple slices evenly over batter. Sprinkle Crumb Topping over apples. Cover; let rise in warm, draft-free place until doubled in size, about 1 hour.

Bake at 375°F for 35 to 40 minutes or until done. Cool in pan 10 minutes. Remove from pan; cool on wire rack. *Makes 1 (9-inch) cake*

Crumb Topping: Combine 1/3 cup sugar, 1/4 cup all-purpose flour, 1 teaspoon ground cinnamon and 3 tablespoons cold butter or margarine. Mix until crumbly.

Tip: For best results with the Crumb Topping use a pastry blender to cut into the cold butter or margarine. Mix all ingredients until coarse crumbs form.

106

Apple Crumb Coffeecake

Fruit & Nut Coffeecake Ring

1 package active dry yeast

¹/₂ cup warm water (115°F)

4 cups all-purpose flour, divided

1 teaspoon salt

1 teaspoon ground cardamom (optional)

¹/₃ cup butter, melted

¹/₃ cup thawed frozen unsweetened apple juice concentrate

3 eggs, divided

¹/₂ cup no-sugar-added apricot fruit spread

1 package (6 ounces) mixed dried fruit, chopped

¹/₂ cup coarsely chopped toasted pecans

1 teaspoon cold water

1. Dissolve yeast in warm water; let stand 10 minutes. In large bowl of electric mixer, combine 3 cups flour, salt and cardamom, if desired. While mixing on low speed with dough hook, gradually blend in yeast mixture, butter, apple juice concentrate and two eggs. Beat 2 minutes at medium speed. Beat in enough remaining flour to form a stiff dough. Continue to beat until dough is smooth and elastic.* Let rest 20 minutes. Roll out dough on lightly floured surface to 22×12-inch rectangle. Spread fruit spread evenly down center of rectangle, leaving 1 inch border along both long sides. Sprinkle fruit bits and nuts evenly over fruit spread. Starting at one long side, roll dough up tightly; pinch seam to seal. Place on greased cookie sheet. Bring ends of roll together to form ring; pinch ends together to seal, using water if necessary. With scissors or sharp knife, make diagonal cuts, about 1 inch apart, into top of ring. Let rise in warm place 30 minutes. (Dough will not double in volume.)

2. Preheat oven to 375°F. Beat together remaining egg and cold water; brush over ring. Bake 25 to 30 minutes or until golden brown. Immediately remove from pan. Cool on wire rack. Serve warm or at room temperature.   *Makes 10 servings*

Dough may be kneaded by hand on lightly floured surface until smooth and elastic, about 10 minutes.

Fruit & Nut Coffeecake Ring

Raspberry Tea Cake

⅓ cup whole almonds, toasted

2 cups all-purpose flour

¾ cup sugar

½ teaspoon salt

½ cup (1 stick) butter

¾ teaspoon baking powder

½ cup milk

½ teaspoon vanilla

1 egg

¾ cup seedless raspberry jam

1. Preheat oven to 350°F. Grease 9-inch round cake pan; set aside.

2. Place almonds in food processor. Process using on/off pulsing action until almonds are ground, but not pasty.

3. Combine flour, sugar and salt in large bowl. Cut in butter with pastry blender or 2 knives until mixture resembles coarse crumbs. Reserve ½ cup flour mixture. Stir almonds and baking powder into remaining flour mixture.

4. Combine milk, vanilla and egg in medium bowl with wire whisk until well blended. Make well in center of flour mixture. Add milk mixture; stir until mixture forms soft dough. Spread half of dough evenly on bottom of prepared pan. Bake 10 minutes.

5. Remove crust from oven. Spread evenly with jam. Drop remaining dough by teaspoonfuls over jam. Sprinkle with reserved flour mixture. Bake 20 to 25 minutes or until golden brown and toothpick inserted in center comes out clean. Cool cake in pan on wire rack 20 minutes. Cut into wedges. Store covered at room temperature.

Makes 10 servings

Raspberry Tea Cake

Maple Nut Twist

1 recipe Sweet Yeast Dough (page 113)
2 tablespoons butter or margarine, melted
2 tablespoons honey
1/2 cup chopped pecans
1/4 cup granulated sugar
2 1/2 teaspoons maple extract, divided
1/2 teaspoon ground cinnamon
1 cup sifted powdered sugar
5 teaspoons milk

1. Prepare Sweet Yeast Dough; let rise as directed. Combine butter and honey in cup; set aside. Combine pecans, granulated sugar, 2 teaspoons maple extract and cinnamon in small bowl. Toss to coat; set aside.

2. Grease 2 baking sheets. Cut dough into quarters. Roll out one piece dough into 9-inch circle on floured surface with floured rolling pin. (Keep remaining dough covered with towel.) Place on prepared baking sheet. Brush half of butter mixture over dough. Sprinkle half of pecan mixture over butter mixture.

3. Roll another piece of dough into 9-inch circle. Place dough over pecan filling, stretching dough as necessary to cover. Pinch edges to seal. Place 1-inch biscuit cutter in center of circle as cutting guide, being careful not to cut through dough. Cut dough into 12 wedges with scissors or sharp knife, from edge of circle to edge of biscuit cutter, cutting through all layers. Pick up wide edge of 1 wedge, twist several times and lay back down on prepared sheet. Repeat twisting procedure with remaining wedges. Repeat with remaining quarters of dough, butter mixture and pecan mixture. Cover coffeecakes with towel. Let rise in warm place or until doubled in bulk.

4. Preheat oven to 350°F. Bake on two racks in oven 20 to 25 minutes or until coffeecakes are golden brown and sound hollow when tapped. (Rotate baking sheets top to bottom halfway through baking.) Remove from baking sheets; cool on wire racks about 30 minutes.

5. Combine powdered sugar, milk and remaining 1/2 teaspoon maple extract in small bowl until smooth. Drizzle over warm coffeecakes.

Makes 24 servings (2 coffeecakes)

Sweet Yeast Dough

4 to 4 1/4 cups all-purpose flour, divided

1/2 cup granulated sugar

2 packages active dry yeast

1 teaspoon salt

3/4 cup milk

1/4 cup (1/2 stick) butter

2 eggs

1 teaspoon vanilla

1. Combine 1 cup flour, sugar, yeast and salt in large bowl; set aside.

2. Combine milk and butter in small saucepan. Heat over low heat until mixture is 120° to 130°F. (Butter does not need to completely melt.)

3. Gradually beat milk mixture into flour mixture with electric mixer at low speed. Increase speed to medium; beat 2 minutes, scraping down side of bowl once.

4. Reduce speed to low. Beat in eggs, vanilla and 1 cup flour. Increase speed to medium; beat 2 minutes, scraping down side of bowl once. Stir in enough additional flour, about 2 cups, with wooden spoon to make soft dough.

5. Turn out dough onto lightly floured surface; flatten slightly. Knead dough about 5 minutes or until smooth and elastic, adding remaining 1/4 cup flour to prevent sticking if necessary.

6. Shape dough into a ball; place in large greased bowl. Turn dough over so that top is greased. Cover with towel; let rise in warm place 1 1/2 to 2 hours or until doubled in bulk.

7. Punch down dough. Knead dough on lightly floured surface 1 minute. Cover with towel; let rest 10 minutes.

Refrigerator Sweet Yeast Dough: Prepare Sweet Yeast Dough as directed in steps 1 through 6, except cover with greased plastic wrap; refrigerate 3 to 24 hours. Punch down dough. Knead dough on lightly floured surface 1 to 2 minutes. Cover with towel; let dough rest 20 minutes before shaping and second rising. (Second rising may take up to 1 1/2 hours.)

Cranberry-Cheese Batter Bread

1 ¼ cups milk

3 cups all-purpose flour

½ cup sugar

1 package active dry yeast

1 teaspoon salt

½ cup (1 stick) butter, chilled

½ cup (4 ounces) cream cheese, chilled

1 cup (3-ounce package) dried cranberries

1. Heat milk in small saucepan over low heat until temperature reaches 120° to 130°F. Grease 8-inch square pan; set aside. Combine flour, sugar, yeast and salt in large bowl.

2. Cut butter and cream cheese into 1-inch chunks; add to flour mixture. Cut in butter and cream cheese with pastry blender until mixture resembles coarse crumbs. Add cranberries; toss. Add warm milk; beat 1 minute or until dough looks stringy. Place batter in prepared pan. Cover with towel; let rise in warm place about 1 hour.

3. Preheat oven to 375°F. Bake 35 minutes or until golden brown.

Makes 1 loaf

Cranberry-Cheese Batter Bread

Festive Yule Loaves

2 ¾ cups all-purpose flour, divided

⅓ cup sugar

1 teaspoon salt

1 package active dry yeast

1 cup milk

½ cup (1 stick) butter

1 egg

½ cup golden raisins

½ cup chopped candied red and green cherries

½ cup chopped pecans

Vanilla Glaze (recipe follows, optional)

1. Combine 1 ½ cups flour, sugar, salt and yeast in large bowl. Heat milk and butter over medium heat until very warm (120° to 130°F). Gradually stir into flour mixture. Add egg. Mix with electric mixer at low speed 1 minute. Beat at high speed 3 minutes, scraping side of bowl frequently. Toss raisins, cherries and pecans with ¼ cup flour in small bowl; stir into yeast mixture. Stir in enough of remaining 1 cup flour to make a soft dough. Turn out onto lightly floured surface. Knead about 10 minutes or until smooth and elastic. Place in greased bowl; turn to grease top of dough. Cover with towel. Let rise in warm, draft-free place about 1 hour or until doubled in bulk.

2. Punch dough down. Divide in half. Roll out each half on lightly floured surface to form 8-inch circle. Fold in half; press only folded edge firmly. Place on ungreased cookie sheet. Cover with towel. Let rise in warm, draft-free place about 30 minutes or until doubled in bulk.

3. Preheat oven to 375°F. Bake 20 to 25 minutes until golden brown. Remove from cookie sheet and cool completely on wire rack. Frost with Vanilla Glaze, if desired. Store in airtight containers.

Makes 2 loaves

Vanilla Glaze: Combine 1 cup sifted powdered sugar, 4 to 5 teaspoons light cream or half-and-half and ½ teaspoon vanilla in small bowl; stir until smooth.

Festive Yule Loaf

Gingerbread House

5 1/4 cups all-purpose flour

1 tablespoon ground ginger

2 teaspoons baking soda

1 1/2 teaspoons allspice

1 teaspoon salt

2 cups packed dark brown sugar

1 cup (2 sticks) plus 2 tablespoons butter, softened and divided

3/4 cup dark corn syrup

2 eggs

Meringue Powder Royal Icing (page 120)

Assorted gumdrops, hard candies and decors

1. Draw patterns for house on cardboard, using diagram on page 120 as guide; cut out patterns. Preheat oven to 375°F. Grease large cookie sheet.

2. Combine flour, ginger, baking soda, allspice and salt in medium bowl.

3. Beat brown sugar and 1 cup butter in large bowl with electric mixer at medium speed until light and fluffy. Beat in corn syrup and eggs. Gradually add flour mixture. Beat at low speed until well blended.

4. Roll about 1/4 of dough directly onto prepared cookie sheet to 1/4-inch thickness. Lay sheet of waxed paper over dough. Place patterns over waxed paper 2 inches apart. Cut dough around patterns with sharp knife; remove waxed paper. Reserve scraps to reroll with next batch of dough.

5. Bake 15 minutes or until no indentation remains when cookie is touched in center. While cookies are still hot, place cardboard pattern lightly over cookie; trim edges to straighten. Let stand on cookie sheet 5 minutes. Remove cookies to wire racks; cool completely. Repeat with remaining pattern pieces.

6. Prepare Meringue Powder Royal Icing. If desired, some icing may be divided into small bowls and tinted with food coloring to use for decorative piping.

7. Cover 12-inch square piece of cardboard with colored paper; use as base for house.

continued on page 120

118

Gingerbread House

Gingerbread House, *continued*

8. Place icing in small resealable plastic food storage bag; cut off small corner of bag. Pipe icing on edges of all pieces including bottom; "glue" house together at seams and onto base.

9. Pipe door, shutters, etc. onto front of house. Decorate as desired with icing and candies. If desired, dust house with sifted powdered sugar to resemble snow.

Makes 1 gingerbread house

Meringue Powder Royal Icing

¹/₄ cup meringue powder*

6 tablespoons water

1 box (16 ounces) powdered sugar, sifted

*Meringue powder is available where cake decorating supplies are sold.

1. Beat meringue powder and water in medium bowl with electric mixer at low speed until well blended. Beat at high speed until stiff peaks form.

2. Beat in sugar at low speed until well blended. Beat at high speed until icing is very stiff. Cover icing with damp cloth to prevent it from drying. Makes about 2½ cups.

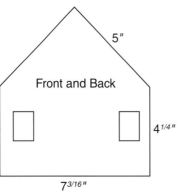

5"

Front and Back

4¹/₄"

7³/₁₆"

Front: Cut 1 pattern for front of house. Cut 2 windows.

Back: Cut 1 pattern for back of house. Cut 2 windows.

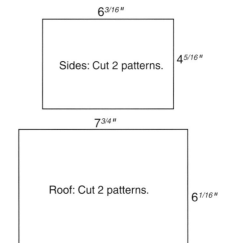

6³/₁₆"

Sides: Cut 2 patterns.

4⁵/₁₆"

7³/₄"

Roof: Cut 2 patterns.

6¹/₁₆"

Cherry Orange Poppy Seed Muffins

- **2** cups all-purpose flour
- **³/₄** cup granulated sugar
- **1** tablespoon baking powder
- **1** tablespoon poppy seeds
- **¹/₄** teaspoon salt
- **1** cup milk
- **¹/₄** cup (¹/₂ stick) butter, melted
- **1** egg, lightly beaten
- **¹/₄** cup tart dried cherries
- **3** tablespoons grated orange peel

Combine flour, sugar, baking powder, poppy seeds and salt in large mixing bowl. Add milk, melted butter and egg, stirring just until dry ingredients are moistened. Gently stir in cherries and orange peel. Fill paper-lined muffin cups three-fourths full.

Bake in preheated 400°F oven 18 to 22 minutes or until wooden pick inserted in center comes out clean. Let cool in pan 5 minutes. Remove from pan and serve warm or let cool completely.

Makes 12 muffins

Favorite recipe from **Cherry Marketing Institute**

 Tips to share

Don't stir muffin batter too much— overmixing will make the muffins tough. There should still be lumps in the batter; these will disappear during baking.

Festive Caramel Floral Rolls

2 cups water

1 cup packed dark brown sugar, divided

1/2 cup shortening

5 1/2 to 6 cups all-purpose flour, divided

2 packages active dry yeast

2 teaspoons *each* salt and baking powder

2 teaspoons vanilla

3 tablespoons butter

3 tablespoons milk

122

1. Heat water, 1/2 cup brown sugar and shortening in small saucepan over medium heat until sugar dissolves and shortening melts. Remove from heat; cool to 120° to 130°F.

2. Combine 3 cups flour, yeast, salt and baking powder in large bowl. Add water mixture and vanilla; beat vigorously 2 minutes. Add remaining flour, 1/4 cup at a time, until dough begins to pull away from side of bowl. Turn out dough onto floured work surface; flatten slightly. Knead 10 minutes or until smooth and elastic, adding flour if necessary to prevent sticking.

3. Shape dough into ball. Place in large lightly oiled bowl; turn dough over once to oil surface. Cover with towel; let rise in warm place about 1 hour or until doubled in bulk.

4. Turn dough out onto lightly oiled work surface. Divide into 24 equal pieces. Form each piece into ball. Cover with towel on work surface; let rest 5 minutes.

5. Preheat oven to 375°F. Lightly grease 2 baking sheets. Roll 12 balls of dough into 10-inch ropes; keeping remaining balls covered. Tie one 10-inch rope into knot. Place in center of prepared baking sheet. Form remaining 11 ropes into tear drop shape so loose ends touch. Place on baking sheet around dough knot to form daisy-like flower. Repeat with remaining dough. Bake 25 minutes or until deep golden brown.

6. While bread is baking, melt butter in small saucepan over medium-low heat. When butter begins to bubble, add remaining 1/2 cup brown sugar; stir 3 minutes. Add milk. Bring to a boil without stirring. Cook 3 minutes; remove from heat and cool.

7. When bread is done baking, immediately remove bread from baking sheet and cool on wire rack. Brush each loaf with butter mixture using pastry brush.

Makes 24 rolls

Festive Caramel Floral Rolls

Holiday Pumpkin Muffins

2 1/2 cups all-purpose flour

1 cup packed light brown sugar

1 tablespoon baking powder

1 teaspoon ground cinnamon

1/2 teaspoon ground nutmeg

1/2 teaspoon ground ginger

1/4 teaspoon salt

1 cup solid-pack pumpkin (not pumpkin pie filling)

3/4 cup milk

2 eggs

6 tablespoons butter, melted

2/3 cup roasted, salted pumpkin seeds, divided

1/2 cup golden raisins

1. Preheat oven to 400°F. Grease or paper-line 18 (2¾-inch) muffin cups.

2. Combine flour, brown sugar, baking powder, cinnamon, nutmeg, ginger and salt in large bowl. Stir pumpkin, milk, eggs and melted butter in medium bowl until well blended. Stir pumpkin mixture into flour mixture. Mix just until all ingredients are moistened. Stir in 1/3 cup pumpkin seeds and raisins. Spoon into prepared muffin cups, filling 2/3 full. Sprinkle remaining pumpkin seeds over muffin batter.

3. Bake 15 to 18 minutes or until toothpick inserted in center comes out clean. Cool in pans 10 minutes. Remove from pans and cool completely on wire racks. Store in airtight container. *Makes 18 muffins*

Holiday Pumpkin Muffins

Toll House® Famous Fudge

1 ½ cups granulated sugar

⅔ cup (5 fluid-ounce can) NESTLÉ® CARNATION® Evaporated Milk

2 tablespoons butter or margarine

¼ teaspoon salt

2 cups miniature marshmallows

1 ½ cups (9 ounces) NESTLÉ® TOLL HOUSE® Semi-Sweet Chocolate Morsels

½ cup chopped pecans or walnuts (optional)

1 teaspoon vanilla extract

LINE 8-inch-square baking pan with foil.

COMBINE sugar, evaporated milk, butter and salt in medium, heavy-duty saucepan. Bring to a full rolling boil over medium heat, stirring constantly. Boil, stirring constantly, for 4 to 5 minutes. Remove from heat.

STIR in marshmallows, morsels, nuts and vanilla extract. Stir vigorously for 1 minute or until marshmallows are melted. Pour into prepared baking pan; refrigerate for 2 hours or until firm. Lift from pan; remove foil. Cut into pieces.   *Makes 49 pieces*

For Milk Chocolate Fudge: SUBSTITUTE 1 ¾ cups (11.5-ounce package) NESTLÉ® TOLL HOUSE® Milk Chocolate Morsels for Semi-Sweet Morsels.

For Butterscotch Fudge: SUBSTITUTE 1 ⅔ cups (11-ounce package) NESTLÉ® TOLL HOUSE® Butterscotch Flavored Morsels for Semi-Sweet Morsels.

For Peanutty Chocolate Fudge: SUBSTITUTE 1 ⅔ cups (11-ounce package) NESTLÉ® TOLL HOUSE® Peanut Butter & Milk Chocolate Morsels for Semi-Sweet Morsels and ½ cup chopped peanuts for pecans or walnuts.

Toll House® Famous Fudge

Christmas Tree Platter

1 recipe Christmas Ornament Cookie Dough (recipe follows)
2 cups sifted powdered sugar
2 tablespoons milk or lemon juice
Assorted food colorings, colored sugars and assorted small decors

1. Preheat oven to 350°F. Prepare Christmas Ornament Cookie Dough. Divide dough in half. Reserve 1 half; refrigerate remaining dough. Roll reserved half of dough to ⅛-inch thickness.

2. Cut out tree shapes with cookie cutters. Place on ungreased cookie sheets.

3. Bake 10 to 12 minutes or until edges are lightly browned. Remove to wire racks; cool completely.

4. Repeat with remaining half of dough. Reroll scraps; cut into small circles for ornaments, squares and rectangles for gift boxes and tree trunks.

5. Bake 8 to 12 minutes, depending on size of cookies.

6. Mix sugar and milk for icing. Tint most of icing green and a smaller amount red or other colors for ornaments and boxes. Spread green icing on trees. Sprinkle ornaments and boxes with colored sugars or decorate as desired. Arrange cookies on flat platter to resemble tree as shown in photo.   *Makes about 1 dozen cookies*

Tip: Use this beautiful Christmas Tree Platter cookie as your centerpiece for this holiday's family dinner. It's sure to receive lots of "oohs" and "ahs!"

Christmas Ornament Cookie Dough

2 ¼ cups all-purpose flour
¼ teaspoon salt
1 cup sugar
¾ cup (1 ½ sticks) butter, softened
1 egg
1 teaspoon vanilla
1 teaspoon almond extract

continued on page 130

Christmas Tree Platter

Christmas Tree Platter, *continued*

1. Combine flour and salt in medium bowl.

2. Beat sugar and butter in large bowl at medium speed of electric mixer until fluffy. Beat in egg, vanilla and almond extract. Gradually add flour mixture. Beat at low speed until well blended.

3. Form dough into 2 discs; wrap in plastic wrap and refrigerate 30 minutes or until firm.

Pumpkin Polka Dot Cookies

1 1/4 cups **EQUAL® SPOONFUL***

1/2 cup (1 stick) butter or margarine, softened

3 tablespoons light molasses

1 cup canned pumpkin

1 egg

1 1/2 teaspoons vanilla

1 2/3 cups all-purpose flour

1 teaspoon baking powder

1 1/4 teaspoons ground cinnamon

1/2 teaspoon ground nutmeg

1/2 teaspoon ground ginger

1/2 teaspoon baking soda

1/4 teaspoon salt

1 cup mini semi-sweet chocolate chips

May substitute 30 packets EQUAL® sweetener.

✦ Beat Equal®, butter and molasses until well combined. Mix in pumpkin, egg and vanilla until blended. Gradually stir in combined flour, baking powder, spices, baking soda and salt until well blended. Stir in chocolate chips.

✦ Drop by teaspoonfuls onto baking sheet sprayed with nonstick cooking spray. Bake in preheated 350°F oven 11 to 13 minutes. Remove from baking sheet; cool completely on wire rack. Store at room temperature in airtight container up to 1 week.

Makes about 4 dozen cookies

Pumpkin Polka Dot Cookies

Molasses Spice Cookies

1 ³/₄ cups all-purpose flour

1 teaspoon baking soda

1 teaspoon ground ginger

1 teaspoon ground cinnamon

¹/₄ teaspoon ground cloves

¹/₄ teaspoon salt

1 cup granulated sugar

³/₄ cup (1 ¹/₂ sticks) butter or margarine, softened

1 egg

¹/₄ cup unsulphured molasses

2 cups (12-ounce package) NESTLÉ® TOLL HOUSE® Premier White Morsels

1 cup finely chopped walnuts

COMBINE flour, baking soda, ginger, cinnamon, cloves and salt in small bowl. Beat sugar and butter in large mixer bowl until creamy. Beat in egg and molasses. Gradually beat in flour mixture. Stir in morsels. Refrigerate for 20 minutes or until slightly firm.

PREHEAT oven to 375°F.

ROLL dough into 1-inch balls; roll in walnuts. Place on ungreased baking sheets.

BAKE for 9 to 11 minutes or until golden brown. Cool on baking sheets for 2 minutes; remove to wire racks to cool completely. *Makes about 2¹/₂ dozen cookies*

132

Candy Cane Cookies

1 1/4 cups granulated sugar

1 Butter Flavor **CRISCO**® Stick or 1 cup Butter Flavor **CRISCO**® all-vegetable shortening

2 eggs

1/4 cup light corn syrup or regular pancake syrup

1 tablespoon vanilla

3 cups plus 4 tablespoons all-purpose flour, divided

3/4 teaspoon baking powder

1/2 teaspoon baking soda

1/2 teaspoon salt

1/2 teaspoon red food color

1/4 teaspoon peppermint extract

1. Combine sugar and 1 cup shortening in large bowl. Beat at medium speed of electric mixer until well blended. Add eggs, syrup and vanilla. Beat until well blended and fluffy.

2. Combine 3 cups flour, baking powder, baking soda and salt. Add gradually to creamed mixture at low speed. Mix until well blended.

3. Divide dough in half. Add red food color and peppermint extract to one half. Wrap each half in plastic wrap. Refrigerate several hours or overnight.

4. Heat oven to 375°F. Place sheets of foil on countertop for cooling cookies.

5. Roll 1 rounded teaspoonful plain dough with hands into a 6-inch rope on lightly floured surface. Repeat, using 1 teaspoonful red dough. Place ropes side by side. Twist together gently. Pinch ends to seal. Curve one end into the "hook" of a candy cane. Transfer to ungreased baking sheet with large pancake turner. Repeat with remaining dough. Place cookies 2 inches apart.

6. Bake one baking sheet at a time at 375°F for 7 to 9 minutes, or until just lightly browned. Do not overbake. Cool 2 minutes on baking sheet. Remove cookies to foil to cool completely.   *Makes about 4 1/2 dozen cookies*

133

Layered Toasted Hazelnut Fudge

1 ½ cups coarsely chopped hazelnuts (8 ounces), divided
  2 cups granulated sugar
  1 cup packed brown sugar
  1 can (5 ounces) evaporated milk (⅔ cup)
  ½ cup (1 stick) butter
  1 jar (7 ounces) marshmallow creme
1 ½ teaspoons vanilla
  ½ teaspoon salt
  6 ounces semisweet chocolate, chopped

1. Preheat oven to 350°F. Line 8-inch square pan with foil, leaving 1-inch overhang on sides. Lightly butter foil.

2. Place 1 cup hazelnuts in food processor. Process until smooth peanut butter consistency is reached; set aside.

3. Spray inside of heavy 4-quart saucepan with nonstick cooking spray. Combine sugars, evaporated milk and butter in saucepan; bring to a full rolling boil over medium heat, stirring frequently to prevent scorching.

4. Attach candy thermometer to side of pan. Continue boiling 5 minutes or until sugar mixture reaches soft-ball stage (238°F) on candy thermometer, stirring constantly. Reduce heat to low; stir in marshmallow creme, vanilla and salt until blended. Remove from heat.

5. Transfer 2 cups sugar mixture to medium bowl; stir in reserved hazelnut paste.

6. Add chocolate to sugar mixture in saucepan; stir until blended. Stir in chopped hazelnuts.

7. Pour chocolate mixture into prepared pan; spread evenly. Pour reserved hazelnut mixtures on top of chocolate mixture; spread evenly.

8. Score into 36 squares while fudge is still warm. Cool completely. Remove from pan by lifting fudge and foil using foil handles. Place on cutting board; cut along score lines into squares. Remove foil.

Makes 3 dozen candies

Layered Toasted Hazelnut Fudge

Bolivian Almond Cookies
(Alfajores de Almendras)

- **4** cups natural almonds
- **1** cup all-purpose flour
- **1/4** teaspoon salt
- **1** cup sugar
- **3/4** cup (**1 1/2** sticks) butter, softened
- **1** teaspoon vanilla extract
- **1/2** teaspoon almond extract
- **2** eggs
- **2** tablespoons milk
- **1** tablespoon grated lemon peel
- **1** cup sliced natural almonds

1. Place 4 cups almonds in food processor. Process using on/off pulsing action until almonds are ground, but not pasty.

2. Preheat oven to 350°F. Grease cookie sheets; set aside.

3. Place ground almonds, flour and salt in medium bowl; stir to combine.

4. Beat sugar, butter, vanilla and almond extracts in large bowl with electric mixer at medium speed until light and fluffy. Beat in eggs and milk. Gradually add 1/2 of flour mixture. Beat at low speed until well blended. Stir in lemon peel and remaining flour mixture.

5. Drop rounded teaspoonfuls of dough 2 inches apart onto prepared cookie sheets. Flatten slightly with spoon; top with sliced almonds.

6. Bake 10 to 12 minutes or until edges are lightly browned. Remove cookies with spatula to wire racks; cool completely. *Makes about 3 dozen cookies*

Bolivian Almond Cookies (Alfajores de Almendras)

Chocolate Chip Cookie Dough Fudge

⅓ cup butter, melted

⅓ cup packed brown sugar

¾ cup all-purpose flour

½ teaspoon salt, divided

1⅓ cups mini semisweet chocolate chips, divided

1 package (1 pound) powdered sugar (about 4 cups)

1 package (8 ounces) cream cheese, softened

1 teaspoon vanilla

1. Line 8- or 9-inch square pan with foil, leaving 1-inch overhang on sides. Lightly butter foil.

2. Combine butter and brown sugar in small bowl. Stir in flour and ¼ teaspoon salt. Stir in ⅓ cup chips.

3. Form dough into ball. Place on plastic wrap; flatten into disc. Wrap disc in plastic wrap; freeze 10 minutes or until firm.

4. Unwrap dough and cut into ½-inch pieces; refrigerate.

5. Place powdered sugar, cream cheese, vanilla and remaining ¼ teaspoon salt in large bowl. Beat with electric mixer at low speed until combined. Scrape down side of bowl; beat at medium speed until smooth.

6. Melt remaining 1 cup chips in heavy small saucepan over very low heat, stirring constantly. Remove from heat as soon as chocolate is melted.

7. Add melted chocolate to cream cheese mixture; beat just until blended. Stir in chilled cookie dough pieces.

8. Spread evenly in prepared pan. Score into squares, about 1¼ × 1¼ inches, while fudge is still warm.

9. Refrigerate until firm. Remove from pan by lifting fudge and foil using foil handles. Place on cutting board; cut along score lines into squares. Remove foil. Store in airtight container in refrigerator. *Makes about 3 to 4 dozen candies*

138

Chocolate Chip Cookie Dough Fudge

Rugelach

1 ½ cups all-purpose flour

¼ teaspoon salt

¼ teaspoon baking soda

½ cup (1 stick) butter, softened

1 package (3 ounces) cream cheese, softened

⅓ cup plus ¼ cup granulated sugar, divided

1 teaspoon grated lemon peel, divided

1 cup ground toasted walnuts*

1 teaspoon ground cinnamon

2 tablespoons honey

1 tablespoon lemon juice

Powdered sugar

To toast walnuts, spread them in single layer on ungreased baking sheet; bake in preheated 350°F oven 8 to 10 minutes or until golden brown, stirring frequently. Remove walnuts from baking sheet to cool. To grind walnuts, place in food processor. Process using on/ off pulsing action until ground, but not pasty.

1. Combine flour, salt and baking soda in small bowl.

2. Beat butter, cream cheese, ⅓ cup granulated sugar and ½ teaspoon lemon peel in large bowl with electric mixer at medium speed about 5 minutes or until light and fluffy. Gradually add flour mixture. Beat at low speed until well blended.

3. Form dough into three 5-inch discs; wrap in plastic wrap and refrigerate until firm, about 2 hours.

4. Preheat oven to 375°F. Grease cookie sheets; set aside.

5. Combine walnuts, remaining ¼ cup granulated sugar and cinnamon in medium bowl; set aside. Combine honey, remaining ½ teaspoon lemon peel and lemon juice in small bowl; set aside.

6. Working with 1 piece of dough at a time, remove plastic wrap and place dough on lightly floured surface. Roll out dough with lightly floured rolling pin to 10-inch circle. Keep remaining dough refrigerated.

continued on page 142

140

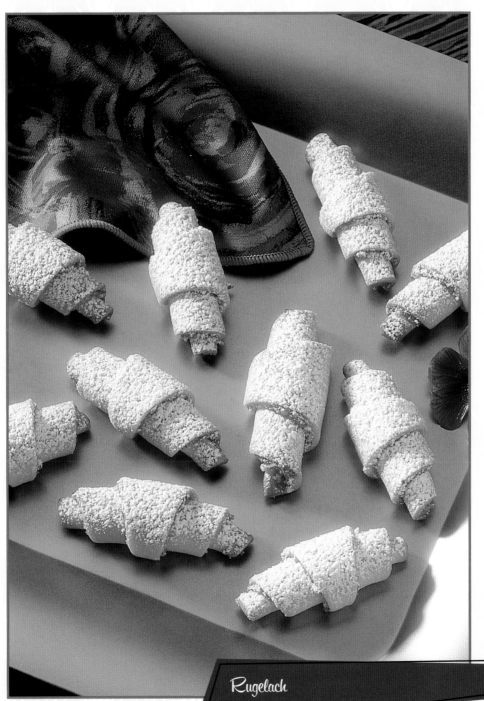

Rugelach

Rugelach, *continued*

7. Brush with ⅓ of honey mixture. Sprinkle with ⅓ cup nut mixture. Lightly press nut mixture into dough.

8. Cut circle into 12 triangles with pizza cutter or sharp knife. Beginning with wide end of triangle, tightly roll up, jelly-roll fashion. Place cookies 1 inch apart on prepared cookie sheet.

9. Repeat with 2 remaining dough pieces and filling ingredients. Bake 10 to 12 minutes or until lightly golden brown. Let cookies stand on cookie sheets 1 minute. Remove cookies to wire racks; cool completely. Sprinkle with powdered sugar. Store tightly covered. *Makes 3 dozen cookies*

Brown Sugar Fudge

1 ⅓ cups granulated sugar
1 ⅓ cups whipping cream
⅔ cup packed brown sugar
1 tablespoon light corn syrup
¼ cup (½ stick) butter
½ cup white chocolate chips
½ cup chopped walnuts

1. Butter 8-inch square pan; set aside. Lightly butter side of heavy, large saucepan.

2. Combine granulated sugar, whipping cream, brown sugar and corn syrup in prepared saucepan. Cook over medium heat, stirring constantly, until sugar dissolves and mixture comes to a boil. Add candy thermometer. Stir mixture occasionally. Continue to cook until mixture reaches soft-ball stage (238°F).

3. Remove from heat. Slice butter into thin slices and place on top of cooling mixture. Let stand about 10 minutes. Add white chocolate chips and nuts. Stir until butter and chips are completely melted. Spread into prepared pan. Refrigerate until firm. Cut into squares. Store in refrigerator. *Makes about 1 pound*

Brown Sugar Fudge

Frosted Holiday Cut-Outs

1 ¹/₄ cups granulated sugar

  1 Butter Flavor **CRISCO**® Stick or 1 cup Butter Flavor **CRISCO**®
all-vegetable shortening

  2 eggs

¹/₄ cup light corn syrup or regular pancake syrup

  1 tablespoon vanilla

  3 cups plus 4 tablespoons all-purpose flour, divided

³/₄ teaspoon baking powder

¹/₂ teaspoon baking soda

¹/₂ teaspoon salt

Icing

  1 cup confectioners' sugar

  2 tablespoons milk

    Food color (optional)

    Decorating icing

1. Combine sugar and 1 cup shortening in large bowl. Beat at medium speed of electric mixer until well blended. Add eggs, syrup and vanilla; beat until well blended and fluffy. Combine 3 cups flour, baking powder, baking soda and salt in medium bowl. Gradually add to shortening mixture, beating at low speed until well blended. Divide dough into 4 equal pieces; shape each into disk. Wrap in plastic wrap. Refrigerate 1 hour until firm.

2. Heat oven to 375°F. Place sheets of foil on countertop for cooling cookies. Sprinkle about 1 tablespoon flour on large sheet of waxed paper. Place disk of dough on floured paper; flatten slightly with hands. Turn dough over; cover with another large sheet of waxed paper. Roll dough to ¹/₄-inch thickness. Remove top sheet of waxed paper. Cut into desired shapes with floured cookie cutters. Place 2 inches apart on ungreased baking sheet. Repeat with remaining dough.

3. Bake one baking sheet at a time at 375°F for 5 to 7 minutes or until edges of cookies are lightly browned. Do not overbake. Cool 2 minutes on baking sheet. Remove cookies to foil to cool completely.

4. For icing, combine confectioners' sugar and milk; stir until smooth. Add food color, if desired. Stir until blended. Spread icing on cookies; place on foil until icing is set. Decorate as desired with decorating icing.   *Makes about 3¹/₂ dozen cookies*

Frosty's Ultimate Chocolate Chip Cookies

1 ¼ cups firmly packed light brown sugar

¾ Butter Flavor CRISCO® Stick or ¾ cup Butter Flavor CRISCO® all-vegetable shortening

2 tablespoons milk

1 tablespoon vanilla

1 egg

1 ¾ cups all-purpose flour

1 teaspoon salt

¾ teaspoon baking soda

2 cups red and green candy-coated chocolate pieces

1. Heat oven to 375°F. Place sheets of foil on countertop for cooling cookies.

2. Combine brown sugar, ¾ cup shortening, milk and vanilla in large bowl. Beat at medium speed of electric mixer until well blended. Beat egg into creamed mixture.

3. Combine flour, salt and baking soda. Mix into creamed mixture just until blended. Stir in candy-coated chocolate pieces.

4. Drop rounded tablespoonfuls of dough 3 inches apart onto ungreased baking sheet.

5. Bake one baking sheet at a time at 375°F for 8 to 10 minutes for chewy cookies, or 11 to 13 minutes for crisp cookies. *Do not overbake.* Cool 2 minutes on baking sheet. Remove cookies to foil to cool completely.   *Makes about 3 dozen cookies*

Fried Norwegian Cookies (Fattigmandbakkelse)

2 eggs, at room temperature

3 tablespoons granulated sugar

¼ cup (½ stick) butter, melted

2 tablespoons milk

I teaspoon vanilla

I ¾ to 2 cups all-purpose flour

Vegetable oil

Powdered sugar

1. Beat eggs and sugar in large bowl with electric mixer at medium speed until thick and lemon colored. Beat in butter, milk and vanilla until well blended. Gradually add 1 ½ cups flour. Beat at low speed until well blended. Stir in enough remaining flour with spoon to form soft dough. Divide dough into 4 portions; cover and refrigerate until firm, at least 2 hours or overnight.

2. Working with floured hands, shape 1 portion dough at a time into 1-inch-thick square. Place dough on lightly floured surface. Roll out dough to 11-inch square. Cut dough into 1 ¼-inch strips; cut strips diagonally at 2-inch intervals. Cut 1 ¼-inch slit vertically down center of each strip. Insert one end of strip through cut to form twist; repeat with each strip. Repeat with remaining dough portions.

3. Heat oil in large saucepan to 365°F. Place 12 cookies at a time in hot oil. Fry about 1 ½ minutes or until golden brown, turning cookies once with slotted spoon. Drain on paper towels. Dust cookies with powdered sugar. Cookies are best if served immediately, but can be stored in airtight container for up to 1 day.

Makes about 11 dozen cookies

Fried Norwegian Cookies (Fattigmandbakkelse)

Christmas Cookie Pops

1 package (20 ounces) refrigerated sugar cookie dough
All-purpose flour (optional)
20 to 24 (4-inch) lollipop sticks
Meringue Powder Royal Icing (page 120)
6 ounces almond bark (vanilla or chocolate) or butterscotch chips
Shortening
Assorted small candies

1. Preheat oven to 350°F. Grease cookie sheets; set aside. Remove dough from wrapper according to package directions.

2. Sprinkle dough with flour to minimize sticking, if necessary. Cut dough in half. Reserve 1 half; refrigerate remaining dough.

3. Roll reserved dough to $\frac{1}{3}$-inch thickness. Cut out cookies using $3\frac{1}{4}$- or $3\frac{1}{2}$-inch Christmas cookie cutters. Place lollipop sticks on cookies so that tips of sticks are imbedded in cookies. Carefully turn cookies with spatula so sticks are in back; place on prepared cookie sheets. Repeat with remaining dough.

4. Bake 7 to 11 minutes or until edges are lightly browned. Cool cookies on sheets 2 minutes. Remove cookies to wire racks; cool completely.

5. Prepare Meringue Powder Royal Icing.

6. Melt almond bark in medium microwavable bowl according to package directions. Add 1 or more tablespoons shortening if coating is too thick. Hold cookies over bowl; spoon coating over cookies. Scrape excess coating from cookie edges. Decorate with small candies and icing immediately. Place cookies on wire racks set over waxed paper; let stand until set. Store in airtight container at room temperature.

Makes 20 to 24 cookies

148

149

Christmas Cookie Pops

Peanut Butter Fudge

1 ½ cups granulated sugar

1 ½ cups packed brown sugar

½ cup milk

1 tablespoon unsweetened cocoa powder

1 cup creamy or chunky peanut butter

½ cup (1 stick) butter

1 teaspoon vanilla

1. Combine sugars, milk and cocoa in large saucepan. Cook over medium heat, stirring constantly, until mixture reaches 238°F (soft ball stage) on candy thermometer.

2. Remove from heat; add peanut butter, butter and vanilla. Stir until melted. Pour into greased 13×9-inch pan (or, use 9×9-inch pan for thicker fudge). Cool completely. Cut into 1-inch squares.   *Makes about 1 ¼ pounds fudge*

Tips to share

For easy clean-up, line pan with foil; butter foil. Simply lift fudge out of pan and cut into pieces.

Peanut Butter Fudge

Chocolate Snowball Cookies

1 cup (2 sticks) butter or margarine, softened
¾ cup packed light brown sugar
1 egg
1 teaspoon vanilla extract
2 cups all-purpose flour
½ cup HERSHEY®'S Dutch Processed Cocoa or HERSHEY®'S Cocoa
1 teaspoon baking powder
¼ teaspoon baking soda
3 tablespoons milk
¾ cup finely chopped macadamia nuts or almonds
¾ cup HEATH® BITS 'O BRICKLE® Toffee Bits
Powdered sugar

1. Beat butter, brown sugar, egg and vanilla in large bowl until blended. Stir together flour, cocoa, baking powder and baking soda; add with milk to butter mixture until well blended. Stir in nuts and toffee.

2. Refrigerate until firm enough to handle, at least 2 hours. Heat oven to 350°F. Shape dough into 1-inch balls; place 2 inches apart on ungreased cookie sheet.

3. Bake 8 to 10 minutes or until set. Remove from cookie sheet to wire rack. Cool completely; roll in powdered sugar.   *Makes about 4 dozen cookies*

Mocha Mint Crisps

1 cup (2 sticks) butter or margarine, softened
1 cup sugar
1 egg
$\frac{1}{4}$ cup light corn syrup
$\frac{1}{4}$ teaspoon peppermint extract
1 teaspoon powdered instant coffee
1 teaspoon hot water
2 cups all-purpose flour
6 tablespoons HERSHEY®'S Cocoa
2 teaspoons baking soda
$\frac{1}{4}$ teaspoon salt
   Mocha Mint Sugar (recipe follows)

1. Beat butter and sugar in large bowl until fluffy. Add egg, corn syrup and peppermint extract; beat until well blended. Dissolve instant coffee in hot water; stir into butter mixture.

2. Stir together flour, cocoa, baking soda and salt; gradually add to butter mixture, beating until well blended. Cover; refrigerate dough until firm enough to shape into balls.

3. Heat oven to 350°F.

4. Shape dough into 1-inch balls. Roll balls in Mocha Mint Sugar. Place on ungreased cookie sheet, about 2 inches apart.

5. Bake 8 to 10 minutes or until no imprint remains when touched lightly. Cool slightly; remove from cookie sheet to wire rack. Cool completely.

Makes about 4 dozen cookies

Mocha Mint Sugar: Stir together $\frac{1}{4}$ cup powdered sugar, 2 tablespoons finely crushed hard peppermint candies (about 6 candies) and 1 $\frac{1}{2}$ teaspoons powdered instant coffee in small bowl.

Acknowledgments

The publisher would like to thank the companies and organizations listed below for the use of their recipes and photographs in this publication.

ACH FOOD COMPANIES, INC.

American Lamb Council

Birds Eye® Foods

Cherry Marketing Institute

Crisco is a registered trademark of The J.M. Smucker Company

Delmarva Poultry Industry, Inc.

Del Monte Corporation

Dole Food Company, Inc.

Eagle Brand® Sweetened Condensed Milk

Equal® sweetener

Fleischmann's® Margarines and Spreads

Fleischmann's® Yeast

Florida's Citrus Growers

Hershey Foods Corporation

The Hidden Valley® Food Products Company

Holland House® is a registered trademark of Mott's, LLP

Lawry's® Foods

McIlhenny Company (TABASCO® brand Pepper Sauce)

Minnesota Cultivated Wild Rice Council

Mott's® is a registered trademark of Mott's, LLP

National Pork Board

National Turkey Federation

Nestlé USA

New York Apple Association, Inc.

Riviana Foods Inc.

StarKist Seafood Company

The Sugar Association, Inc.

Reprinted with permission of Sunkist Growers, Inc.

Wisconsin Milk Marketing Board

Index

155

Index

Index

METRIC CONVERSION CHART

VOLUME MEASUREMENTS (dry)

1/8 teaspoon = 0.5 mL
1/4 teaspoon = 1 mL
1/2 teaspoon = 2 mL
3/4 teaspoon = 4 mL
1 teaspoon = 5 mL
1 tablespoon = 15 mL
2 tablespoons = 30 mL
1/4 cup = 60 mL
1/3 cup = 75 mL
1/2 cup = 125 mL
2/3 cup = 150 mL
3/4 cup = 175 mL
1 cup = 250 mL
2 cups = 1 pint = 500 mL
3 cups = 750 mL
4 cups = 1 quart = 1 L

VOLUME MEASUREMENTS (fluid)

1 fluid ounce (2 tablespoons) = 30 mL
4 fluid ounces (1/2 cup) = 125 mL
8 fluid ounces (1 cup) = 250 mL
12 fluid ounces (1 1/2 cups) = 375 mL
16 fluid ounces (2 cups) = 500 mL

WEIGHTS (mass)

1/2 ounce = 15 g
1 ounce = 30 g
3 ounces = 90 g
4 ounces = 120 g
8 ounces = 225 g
10 ounces = 285 g
12 ounces = 360 g
16 ounces = 1 pound = 450 g

DIMENSIONS

1/16 inch = 2 mm
1/8 inch = 3 mm
1/4 inch = 6 mm
1/2 inch = 1.5 cm
3/4 inch = 2 cm
1 inch = 2.5 cm

OVEN TEMPERATURES

250°F = 120°C
275°F = 140°C
300°F = 150°C
325°F = 160°C
350°F = 180°C
375°F = 190°C
400°F = 200°C
425°F = 220°C
450°F = 230°C

BAKING PAN SIZES

Utensil	Size in Inches/Quarts	Metric Volume	Size in Centimeters
Baking or Cake Pan (square or rectangular)	8×8×2	2 L	20×20×5
	9×9×2	2.5 L	23×23×5
	12×8×2	3 L	30×20×5
	13×9×2	3.5 L	33×23×5
Loaf Pan	8×4×3	1.5 L	20×10×7
	9×5×3	2 L	23×13×7
Round Layer Cake Pan	8×1½	1.2 L	20×4
	9×1½	1.5 L	23×4
Pie Plate	8×1¼	750 mL	20×3
	9×1¼	1 L	23×3
Baking Dish or Casserole	1 quart	1 L	—
	1½ quart	1.5 L	—
	2 quart	2 L	—